Moral Education and Environmental Concern

This volume explores both some important ways in which moral values are embedded in much current discussion of environmental issues, as well as ways in which some conventional understandings of morality and moral education can be transformed by ideas that have emerged in the discourse of environmental concern. Contributions range from a variety of disciplines including philosophy, psychoanalysis, social psychology, and anthropology, and reflect a variety of cultural settings including Occidental, Oriental, African, and South American. The book discusses the moral character of our relationship with the natural world; the quality of the relationship between our 'internal' and 'external' worlds; the issues that arise when responsibilities towards future generations are considered; and the need for cultural change and the practical obstacles to achieving this in a school context. In the process, insights are drawn from Western philosophy, Buddhism, Daoism, Ubuntu, and Confucianism. The result is a collection that provides a rich backcloth for understanding, and in some cases reconceptualising, morality in an age of growing environmental concern, and its extensive implications for the theory and conduct of moral education.

This book was originally published as a special issue of the *Journal of Moral Education.*

Michael Bonnett has held senior teaching and research posts in the Universities of Bath, Cambridge, and London, UK. He has written extensively in the field of the philosophy of environmental education, with particular reference to ideas of sustainability and education for sustainable development. His book *Retrieving Nature: Education for a Post-Humanist Age* (2004) explores the radical potential of environmental concern for contemporary education.

Moral Education and Environmental Concern

Edited by
Michael Bonnett

Routledge
Taylor & Francis Group
LONDON AND NEW YORK

First published 2014
by Routledge
2 Park Square, Milton Park, Abingdon, Oxfordshire OX14 4RN

and by Routledge
711 Third Avenue, New York, NY 10017

First issued in paperback 2015

Routledge is an imprint of the Taylor & Francis Group, an informa business

British Library Cataloguing in Publication Data
A catalogue record for this book is available from the British Library

ISBN 13: 978-1-138-95378-9 (pbk)
ISBN 13: 978-0-415-72569-9 (hbk)

Typeset in Times New Roman
by Taylor & Francis Books

Publisher's Note
The publisher accepts responsibility for any inconsistencies that may have arisen during the conversion of this book from journal articles to book chapters, namely the possible inclusion of journal terminology.

Contents

Citation Information

The chapters in this book were originally published in the *Journal of Moral Education*, volume 41, issue 3 (September 2012). When citing this material, please use the original page numbering for each article, as follows:

Introduction
Editorial
Michael Bonnett
Journal of Moral Education, volume 41, issue 3 (September 2012) pp. 279-284

Chapter 1
Environmental concern, moral education and our place in nature
Michael Bonnett
Journal of Moral Education, volume 41, issue 3 (September 2012) pp. 285-300

Chapter 2
Questioning the idea of the individual as an autonomous moral agent
C.A. Bowers
Journal of Moral Education, volume 41, issue 3 (September 2012) pp. 301-310

Chapter 3
Reclaiming our moral agency through healing: a call to moral, social, environmental activists
Heesoon Bai
Journal of Moral Education, volume 41, issue 3 (September 2012) pp. 311-328

Chapter 4
Ubuntu, ukama, *environment and moral education*
Lesley Le Grange
Journal of Moral Education, volume 41, issue 3 (September 2012) pp. 329-340

Chapter 5
Some implications for moral education of the Confucian principle of harmony: learning from sustainability education practice in China
Ling Feng and Derek Newton
Journal of Moral Education, volume 41, issue 3 (September 2012) pp. 341-352

Chapter 6

Four slogans for cultural change: an evolving place-based, imaginative and ecological learning experience
Sean Blenkinsop
Journal of Moral Education, volume 41, issue 3 (September 2012) pp. 353-368

Chapter 7

Mountain guides: between ethics and socioeconomic trends
Thierry Long, Damien Bazin and Bernard Massiéra
Journal of Moral Education, volume 41, issue 3 (September 2012) pp. 369-388

Chapter 8

Promoting ethical and environmental awareness in vulnerable communities: a research action plan
Ulisses Araújo
Journal of Moral Education, volume 41, issue 3 (September 2012) pp. 389-398

Chapter 9

Like a swallow, moving forward in circles: on the future dimension of environmental care and education
Dirk Willem Postma and Paul Smeyers
Journal of Moral Education, volume 41, issue 3 (September 2012) pp. 399-412

Please direct any queries you may have about the citations to clsuk.permissions@cengage.com

Notes on Contributors

Ulisses Araújo, PhD, is full Professor of Psychology and Education at the School of Arts, Sciences and Humanities of the University of São Paulo, Brazil, heading the Interdisciplinary Research Center for Complexity and Citizenship. Since 2003 he has been a special consultant to the Brazilian Ministry of Education for the Ethics and Citizenship Program: constructing values at school and in the society, a nationwide moral education program. For three years he has held a Productivity Research Fellowship of the National Council of Scientific and Technological Development (CNPq). Since 1996 he has published 13 books and 21 book chapters in Brazil and Spain, all related to the psychological and educational development of morality, citizenship and human rights.

Heesoon Bai was born in Korea, and immigrated to Canada when she was 18. She obtained her PhD from the University of British Columbia, Canada, in Philosophy of Education in 1996. She is now a Professor in Philosophy of Education, and she teaches and researches in ethics, epistemology, ecology and Eastern philosophies. As an Asian-Canadian researcher, she is active in East–West dialogue, and promotes cross-cultural, worldview-based, and comparative philosophies in education. She served as the Editor of *Paideusis*, the Canadian Journal of the Philosophy of Education Society from 2005 to 2010.

Damien Bazin, PhD in Economics, is Assistant Professor (Accreditation to Supervise Research) in Economics at the University of Nice Sophia Antipolis, France. After postdoctoral studies in Canada and projects in China as part of a European Union program, he joined GREDEG (the Research Group on Lawn Economics and Management). He is conducting research on macroeconomics and sustainable development and, in addition, his fields of specialisation include ecology, ethical and environmental economy and corporate ethics. He develops projects which have direct applications within ecological economics and game theory and regularly collaborates with national daily papers to popularise fundamental research. His latest works are related to the protection of nature and to economic ethics.

Sean Blenkinsop is an Associate Professor of Education at Simon Fraser University, Vancouver, Canada. His research interests include: philosophy of education, school change and the environment. He is the 'primary' investigator on the environmental school project described in this paper.

Michael Bonnett, until recently, was Reader in Philosophy of Education at the University of Bath, UK, and Senior Research Fellow at the University of London Institute of Education, UK. Prior to that he was Senior Lecturer in Philosophy of Education in the University of Cambridge, UK. He has written numerous papers on education published in academic journals and edited books, including several on sustainability and environmental education, and also on personal authenticity, selfhood and emplacement. His book on environmental concern and education, *Retrieving Nature: Education for a Post-Humanist Age*, was published in 2004. His earlier book *Children's Thinking* (1994) explored the significance of a poetic dimension to human understanding and the conduct of education.

C.A. (Chet) Bowers is now semi-retired, but continues to write and to speak to international audiences on the nature of ecological reforms that promote sustainable forms of ecological intelligence, the revitalisation of the cultural commons, and the understanding of the cultural languaging processes that are still being ignored in thinking about sustainable educational reforms. His most recent books are *The false promises of constructivist theories of learning (2005), Perspectives on the ideas of Gregory Bateson, ecological intelligence, and educational reforms* (2011), *University reform in an era of global warming* (2011), and *The way forward* (2012).

Ling Feng, PhD, is a Lecturer in the International Human Resource Research Office of the Chinese Academy of Personnel Science, Beijing, China. Her research interests include environmental education, green job, human resource development. She has published over 30 journal articles and book chapters in English and Chinese including 'Teacher and student responses to interdisciplinary aspects of sustainability education: what do we really know?', *Environmental Education Research* (2012, 18(1)); 'Effortless action: the ability to fulfil human needs effortlessly through working with nature, in A. Stibbe (Ed.) *Handbook of sustainability literacy: skills for a changing world* (2009); 'Cambridge phenomenon: an example of talent innovation and regional economic development', *China Personnel* (6 January, 2012).

Lesley Le Grange is a Professor and Vice-Dean (Research) in the Faculty of Education at Stellenbosch University, South Africa. He teaches and researches in the fields of environmental education, research methodology, science education and curriculum assessment. His most recent research interest is in exploring the nexus of African traditional values, environment and education. He has more than 140 publications and serves on the editorial boards of several peer-reviewed journals.

Thierry Long is a Lecturer at the University of Nice, France, teaching in the Department of Sport Sciences and researching in the laboratory of cognitive and social anthropology and psychology in the Human and Social Sciences Institute. He has published a dozen international articles about ethics and sport, among them 'Institutionalisation versus self-regulation: a contextual analysis of responsibility among adolescent sportsmen', *Journal of Moral Education* (2008, 37(4)). The same year he published a book, *Education through sport: fake or reality.* His main interest is to analyse the moral impact of different contexts of sport practices (such as competitive, self-organised, outdoor activities, adapted physical activities) on practitioners.

Bernard Massiéra, PhD in Communication, is Associate Professor in the Faculty of Sport Sciences, Nice University, France, where he is Advisor on the Masters Course in the Management of Sport and Outdoor Tourism. He is also a member of Laboratory Human Motricity, Education, Sport, Health (LAMHESS). His work focuses on social determinants in sport tourism practices and the forms of social regulations of their organisation. His recent co-authored publications have appeared in the journals, *Sport in Society, Journal of Coastal Conservation* and *European Studies in Sports History.*

Derek Newton (MA) is a former senior lecturer in the School of Education and Professional Development at the University of Huddersfield, UK. He has taught extensively at higher education level in China and the Middle East. He has written widely on educational policy and practice in the UK and other countries. His current interests include power and discourse in the ancient world, with a particular focus on the concepts of 'harmony' in Plato and Confucius.

Dirk Willem Postma is Lecturer in Creative Community Development at HU University of Applied Sciences, Utrecht, The Netherlands. In 2004 he obtained his PhD on the ethical and politico-philosophical dimensions of environmental responsibility and education, later published as *Why care for nature?* (2006). In addition, he has published research papers in the field of social aesthetics, on the themes of citizenship, community arts and cultural interventions in deprived neighbourhoods. His current research interests include environmental education, child's play, social creativity and processes of self-organisation.

Paul Smeyers is full Research Professor for Philosophy of Education at Ghent University and part-time at KU Leuven, The Netherlands. He teaches philosophy of education and methodology of the Geisteswissenschaften. He has published widely on analytical philosophy of education, postmodernism, including such issues as cosmopolitanism and the ethics of care. He is President of the International Network of Philosophers of Education (INPE) and chair of the Research Community Philosophy and History of the Discipline of Education (Research Foundation Flanders, Belgium, FWO-Vlaanderen). Together with Marc Depaepe he has co-edited several books published by the Research Community (Dordrecht, Springer), and with Michael Peters and Nick Burbules he has co-authored *Showing and doing: Wittgenstein as a pedagogical philosopher* (2008).

Introduction

Michael Bonnett
University of Cambridge, UK

A central aim of this special issue of the journal is to illustrate, through a range of disciplinary perspectives and cultural settings, something of the potential significance of environmental concern for moral education. While it is widely recognised that environmental issues and ideas, such as sustainable development, are shot through with moral values, it is not always equally well recognised that moral values and moral education can be radically appraised from an environmental perspective and that initiatives arising out of environmental concern and debate can inaugurate new approaches to moral education, or add particular impetus to existing ones. Some 13 years ago in an introduction to a collection of papers on environmental education and sustainability, John Elliott and I wrote: 'At this stage in its history it would be difficult indeed to identify an issue of greater importance for humankind than its relationship with its environment'.[1] Current global economic concerns might seem to have eclipsed this, but a reduced public profile does nothing to diminish the importance of the underlying issues or the urgency of our situation, which for many have always included not simply prudential considerations resulting from various forms of environmental degradation, but also ethical and spiritual ones concerning what should be the essential character of our relationship with the natural world.

In *The republic* and *The laws*, Plato (2007, 2005 editions) argued that a central aim of education was the development of good citizens—individuals who both recognised themselves as part of a greater whole and their part in contributing to the good of this greater whole. The notion of an internal connection between the good life of the individual and some greater good is central to many forms of morality and one strand of environmental concern lies very much in this tradition; it seeks to develop a more comprehensive notion of what the greater good consists in than is often held to be the case (at least in Western thought) by extending ideas of moral value and membership of the moral community in ways not conventionally conceived. It also firmly roots moral life in this greater whole, insisting that moral conduct is part of a way of being such that it is intimately bound up with our modes of perception, understanding and aesthetic sensibility. These are mutually conditioning and it can be perceived as unhelpful to attempt to draw hard distinctions between them. Thus located, issues highly pertinent to moral education can be discussed without explicit reference to it. With moral conduct and the environment (be it 'inner' psychological, 'outer' social, natural, physical, or geographical) being understood as deeply interfused, a key contemporary concern is with a struggle to achieve a cultural milieu in which a new morality can flourish.

This general theme is indicative of the way in which several of the papers in this issue either argue for, or assume, the need for quite a radical reappraisal of what in the West, at least, can be regarded as some dominant assumptions of moral culture and education. They invite a critical examination of the ontological, epistemological and ethical bases of much current educational practice: the character of the realities that educational institutions invite their members to participate in and celebrate. In this examination, what are taken as aggressive and manipulative aspects of modern rationality are revealed and the essential instrumentalism and economism which is seen as now pervading educational institutions—with their attendant emphases on pre-specification of content, standardised assessment, managerialist organisation and ethos—are severely challenged by the ideas of emergent education that arise or are implicit in many of the papers. This relates to a range of dimensions and issues relevant to moral education not directly taken up in this special issue, but that form part of a broader context that it might be helpful to briefly sample here.

For example, there is the dimension of socio-political issues concerning social justice and the possible vulnerability of liberal democracy as a form of government and way of life. With regard to social justice, arguments have been mounted concerning the environmental racism and class discrimination detected in the ways in which deleterious environmental consequences of Western style economies fall disproportionately on ethnically and economically marginalised communities, for example in coping with climate change, the despoliation caused by resource extraction, and the treatment of exported toxic waste. Threats to the idea of liberal democracy have been identified as being presented by 'ecological imperatives' that arise from the perceived seriousness and urgency of our environmental situation and that might encourage the establishment of an authoritarian technocracy as a response. Resonances of this can be reflected in the school context in a tension between what has been termed 'environmentalism' that focuses on modifying behaviour in ways that have been officially prescribed as environmentally friendly and a fear of bypassing students' personal understanding and critical evaluation of underlying issues (that might lead to a rejection of some of this behaviour).

Because of the nationally and geographically transgressive nature of many burgeoning environmental problems an impetus has been given to considering ideas of global citizenship and the values and attitudes that should inform it—which might differ significantly from those celebrated by a global community founded on trade or some notion of universal human rights. Related to this are issues concerning the possibility of formulating a basic environmental ethic that regulates our conduct in respect of the natural world and that might parallel a basic human ethic, such as that expressed in the UN Charter of Human Rights.[2] This in turn, can hinge on ongoing debates over anthropocentrism versus eco- or bio-centrism as ethical positions and the moral implications of viewing the individual increasingly as part of some greater ecological whole, perhaps such that their good becomes considered to be subordinate to it. Moral aspects of such issues as speciesism (in the sense of unjustifiably privileging human interests over those of other species) and addressing human population growth can become prominent here. A common concern throughout much of such debate is the basic character and extent of human (moral) responsibility when the consequences of human action on the environment can be so extended, both geographically and in time-scale, as often to outrun our current state of knowledge—hence the frequent espousal of some version of the 'precautionary principle' (that emphasises risk avoidance in decision-making where there is uncertainty over consequences), and its restraining implications for how we conceive the 'good life'. For many 'green' thinkers humankind's increasing power to exercise 'dominion over the Earth' has been an ecological disaster and the prospect of their attempting further to 'manage' natural systems is perceived as another instantiation of hubristic humanism that is either to be entertained with deep foreboding or dismissed with heavy irony.[3]

In addition to the background sketched above, it can be helpful to be alert to differing meanings given to central terms used to articulate some of the arguments. For example, in the papers presented in this issue 'environment' can sometimes refer to the biophysical (more or less as directly experienced), or to nested ecosystems, or to the cultural milieu, or to an individual's life-world. 'Ecological' can refer to (again) nested ecosystems, but also can be used as a metaphor for interdependence, or to refer to a way of thinking. And it can be helpful to distinguish between 'sustainable development' conceived as a *policy* that attempts to meld ideas of conservation and development and 'sustainability' conceived as a *frame of mind* or *way of being* in which an individual or culture express particular attitudes and values in their everyday thought and conduct towards the environment.

Turning now to the papers that comprise this special issue: the first paper illustrates the previously mentioned general theme of a need for cultural change. It argues that some strands of environmental concern and ideas regarding the character of our place in nature require a radical review of some dominant understandings of moral education on the grounds that they have too limited and anthropocentric a view of the moral community. It argues that receptivity to a normative character inherent in encounters with nature reveals an enriched terrain for the development of moral sensibility in which intimations of a transcendent other are in play and that challenge a current metaphysical climate of mastery that leads to exploitation of both the human and the non-human.

C.A. Bowers' paper examines the way in which tacitly inherited metaphors that were shaped by earlier and now redundant patterns of thinking reproduce what he argues to be the myth of the autonomous moral agent. Insofar as developing moral autonomy remains an influential aim of moral education in the West, his argument that such autonomy stands in the way of individuals exercising their 'ecological intelligence' in a manner that properly takes account of the interdependent nature of cultural and natural ecologies suggests a radical re-conceptualisation of this aspect of moral education.

Taking up the theme of moral agency, Heesoon Bai argues for an essential link between human destruction of the environment and internal human dystopia that gives rise to an alienation that compromises moral agency. Drawing on Asian philosophies, she explores the project of reclaiming moral agency by overcoming a number of enduring conceptual dichotomies such as those of mind/body and mind/matter and developing a culture of healing centred on more holistic forms of wisdom and compassion.

In his paper examining African traditional values, Lesley Le Grange develops an interpretation of *ubuntu* that brings out a non-speciesist strand of thinking that connects becoming fully human with caring for the entire biophysical world. He argues that it becomes incumbent on moral educators to inform students of their responsibilities to both human and non-human communities and to encourage them to act in the interests of other species by (re-)connecting them to their local environments as active learners and responsible participants. He goes on to illustrate the implications of this in the context of post-apartheid curriculum policy in South Africa.

Ling Feng and Derek Newton discuss how the concept of 'harmony' drawn from Confucian thinking and that arises in the context of Chinese government sustainability education, appropriately interpreted can have significant implications for moral education and indeed, illustrates how moral education and sustainability education are closely related.

Sean Blenkinsop's paper reports on a practical attempt to bring about cultural change stimulated by environmental concern. It discusses the principles and slogans that evolved in the course of, and that helped to orientate, preparatory work in setting up a new school in which the human and the 'more than human' are integrated in its learning culture. As such it foregrounds a range of important ideas and issues involved in an attempt to radically challenge and change the underlying cultural context of moral values and moral education, noting both how the new school is to be structured and its effects on the participants. Here moral values are seen as arising in the context of the activity of envisioning the new school rather than as pre-determining it and hence to a significant degree are grown in a particular context rather than functioning as pre-established imported generalisations.

In their paper Thierry Long, Damien Bazin and Bernard Massiéra examine some of the ethical tensions experienced by those involved in informal moral education in their roles as mountain guides. Their study exemplifies ways in which the widely held aspiration for sport to be a positive socialising influence is compromised by the reality of the larger social climate in which it occurs and in which economic, technical, hedonistic and ecological issues have to be combined and professional responsibilities can become confused. The ways in which a supervening social–economic context can compromise the enactment of moral sentiments has clear parallels for those concerned with moral education in other contexts.

Attention to environmental concern can lend impetus to important approaches to conducting research into moral education. In his paper, Ulisses Araújo describes the strategies being developed in a large research project being undertaken in Brazil in which a focus on sustainability leads to an intervention research program in vulnerable communities that is orientated around drawing school and community together to construct 'moral atmosphere'. The interweaving of ethical and environmental awareness illustrates an important dimension to the embedded nature of moral education in contemporary times.

In the final paper in this collection, Dirk Willem Postma and Paul Smeyers address the issue of moral obligation to future generations. After identifying some of the difficulties that arise here, they explore an approach to environmental education that takes inspiration from the quality of caring taken to be displayed in children's play in nature which, they argue, can stimulate us to think beyond the ethics of self-restraint, with which environmentalism is generally associated, to one that is more motivational and adventurous rather than repressive and precautionary. Importantly, they detect in child play a horizon of 'spiral time' that has significant implications for the character of moral responsibility for the future whose focus becomes immediate caring involvements rather than long-term goals of means-ends reasoning: 'caring for a nearby future that allows us to continue caring'.

In closing this editorial, as guest editor, I would like to express my appreciation for the unstinting advice and support given by Monica Taylor, retiring editor of the journal. Her contribution 'behind the scenes' has been invaluable—not least, her patient and careful final editing of the papers for publication. Also, both for myself and on behalf of those whose work comprises this special issue, I would like to express gratitude to those who reviewed papers. Their thoughtful and often extensive comments have been of immense help to authors in clarifying and developing their thinking. Thanks therefore go to: Kevin Behrens, University of the Witwatersrand, South Africa; Gerte Biesta, University of Stirling, UK; Ian Frowe, University of Cambridge, UK; Joseph Gaie, University of Botswana, Botswana; María Cristina Moreno-Gutiérrez, Universidad de Monterrey, Mexico; Graham Haydon, University of London, Institute of Education, UK; Bob Jickling, Lakehead University, Canada; Jong-ho Joh, Korea National Sports University, South Korea; Hueyli Li, University of Akron, Ohio, USA; Lars Lovlie, University of Oslo, Norway; Catherine Naepflin, University of Freiburg, Germany; Steve Olivier, University of Abertay, Dundee, UK; Richard Smith, University of Durham, UK; Andrew Stables, University of Bath, UK; Christine Winter, University of Sheffield, UK; Teresa Yurent, Universidad Autonoma del Estado de Morelas, Mexico.

Notes

1. Bonnett, M. & Elliott, J. (1999). Editorial. *Cambridge Journal of Education*, Special Issue: Environmental education, sustainability and the transformation of schooling, *29*(3), 309.
2. See, for example, *The Universal Declaration of Rights of Mother Earth* adopted by World People's Conference on Climate Change and the Rights of Mother Earth on 22 April 2010, in Bolivia and submitted to the United Nations for consideration (available online at: www.pwccc.wordpress.com; accessed 28 April 2012).
3. Given its keen awareness of what is taken to be human-induced climate change, species extinction, habitat destruction and pollution that has accompanied human 'progress' (particularly industrialisation), this sentiment implicitly informs a great deal of green thinking. It is expressed more explicitly in, for example, Foreman (1993), Lovelock (2009), Marshall (1995, p. 448) and O'Riordan (1981, p. 1).

References

Foreman, D. (1993). Putting the Earth first. In S. Armstrong & R. Botzler (Eds.), *Environmental ethics*. New York: McGraw-Hill.
Lovelock, J. (2009). *The vanishing face of Gaia*. New York: Basic Books.
Marshall, P. (1995). *Nature's web. Rethinking our place on Earth*. London: Cassell.
O'Riordan, T. (1981). *Environmentalism*. London: Pion.
Plato (2005). *The laws*, Trans. T. J. Saunders. London: Penguin Classics.
Plato (2007). *The republic*, Trans. H. D. P. Lee. London: Penguin Classics.

Environmental concern, moral education and our place in nature

Michael Bonnett
University of Cambridge, UK

Some strands of environmental concern invite a radical re-evaluation of many taken for granted assumptions of late modern ways of life—particularly those that structure how we relate to the natural world. This article explores some of the implications of such a re-evaluation for our understanding of moral education by examining the significance of ideas of our place in nature that focus not on our location in some grand abstract system, but on our felt sense of place in the course of our daily existence. It will be argued that exploration of the anticipatory and ecstatic nature of such concrete emplacement reveals an underlying normative character to our encounters with nature, now experienced as an autonomous and essentially mysterious non-human other that both sustains and is sustained by places—places in which find ourselves and live out our lives. It is argued that this view foregrounds a notion of transcendence that leads to both a questioning of the anthropocentrism (i.e. its metaphysical basis) that informs many Western moral views and an acknowledgement of intrinsic value in nature, such that some current mainstream understandings of the character of moral sensibility and of moral education can no longer be regarded as adequate.

Introduction

Broadly speaking, and from a Western perspective, there are perhaps two chief ways of responding to what is now widely recognised as an increasingly serious set of environmental problems. The first is to seek to develop technical solutions and to attempt to modify behaviour in ways that have minimal impact on our current underlying conceptions of the good life. The second is to see these problems as a manifestation of a need to fundamentally change our underlying conceptions of the good life—and hence of moral education. Although, clearly, in practice at times the two responses will overlap, for present purposes it will be helpful to draw the distinction.

The first response recognises that because of the serious consequences to human well-being of such things as resource depletion, pollution, reduction of biodiversity, we cannot simply go on as we are. We must adapt to changing circumstances in the sense of revising the means by which we achieve current ends, for example by finding new ways of maintaining the economic growth upon which our current way of life depends. This approach has the advantage of least (if nonetheless considerable) disruption to current expectations and aspirations, and hence possesses short-term political expediency. It should be noted that on this view, while we experience environmental problems most acutely in the economic and social spheres, at the bottom there remains a sense in which it is the state of natural systems that provokes the issues. For example, if fossil fuel reserves were much larger than they are believed to be and carbon emissions did not cause planetary warming, a whole dimension of environmental concern would evaporate. As it is, we have to adjust to such inconvenient facts, but on this view not thereby change our underlying relationship with the natural world. Simply, we must learn to exploit it more intelligently.

The second approach views environmental concern as an indicator of a deeper malaise in our current ways of going about things, that is to say that essentially it interprets this concern not as a set of social and economic problems born of the limitations of natural systems, but as an ethical and metaphysical problem concerning the character of our relationship with nature and the world. On this view the circumspection provoked by the prospect of running out of oil or of global warming invites a much deeper level of analysis and response in which both our fundamental motivations towards the natural world and what we assume to be its essential character are put into question. This is to say that the overarching metaphysical climate in which we operate comes up for review.[1]

Because morality always occurs within a particular metaphysical setting, these two stances have differing implications for morality and moral education. On the first approach the character and status of such notions as respect for persons, freedom, equality and human rights in general remain basically the same; their essential individualism and anthropocentrism are simply to be re-expressed in a changing context. On the second approach the nature and operation of such moral values needs re-evaluation because the character of their individualism and the extent of their anthropocentrism no longer seem tenable, perceived, as they become to be, as embedded in a transgressive metaphysics of mastery that ultimately underwrites exploitation of both the human and the non-human. It will be the business of this article to explore some of the dimensions of this re-evaluation and its implications for moral education. In particular, this will be approached from the perspective of what is taken to be a central emerging consideration: our place in nature.

Before proceeding, a caveat needs to be entered concerning the language used in this paper. Language conditions what can be said, therefore insofar as this article aspires to disrupt some conventional (Western) ideas concerning the nature of morality, it should come as no surprise that on occasion I find it necessary to deviate from mainstream academic ways of expressing ideas. Indeed, the need for such a change of lexicon and sometimes of grammar is part of the argument.

Our place in nature

There have been times when the idea of nature and our place in it have been at the forefront of our understanding of ourselves and how we should behave. Eighteenth-century Europe is an example of this, famously captured by Alexander Pope when, in a proto-Romantic moment, he wrote:

> First follow NATURE, and your judgment frame
> By her just Standard ...
> (*An Essay on Criticism*, lines 68–69, in Butt, 1963, p. 146)

A century later the 'non-Romantic' T.H. Huxley, influenced by Darwinism, also acknowledged the significance of nature when he wrote:

> The question of questions for mankind—the problem that underlies all others, and is more deeply interesting than any other—is the ascertainment of the place which Man occupies in nature and his relationship to the universe of things. (cited in Marshall, 1995, p. 319)

To be sure, this concern with nature that was so prominent in eighteenth- and nineteenth-century Europe and North America has many precursors, some ancient. For example, Taoism of sixth-century BC China was concerned to achieve a life that followed nature by reflecting the natural flow of things in their creative spontaneity. In the European context, ideas of 'Earth Mother' were powerful in the mediaeval and early Renaissance world. And of course from time immemorial respect for nature and the requirement to live in harmony with it have been central to the culture of many indigenous peoples.

Having said this, clearly there are important questions to be asked concerning how we are to understand 'nature' (see, for example, Bonnett, 2004; Soper, 1995). In recent times under the influence of post-modernism, ideas of nature and a natural order (along with much else) have become regarded by some simply as social constructs that have little cultural or historical stability and that frequently have served politically to legitimate essentially arbitrary power relationships (see, for example, Haraway, 1991). Yet, there are arguments to suggest that at a certain level, with regard to nature, things are not as ungrounded as this view supposes. For example, the idea of a realm that we experience as essentially independent of human intention has a very long and enduring heritage and its characterisation as spontaneously 'of itself' and in this sense 'self-arising' is to be found both in Taoism and the ancient Greek notion of '*phusis*' (see Heidegger, 1977, p. 10). Elsewhere, I have argued that such a characterisation is still central to how nature is experienced by many in modern times and that it is deeply embedded in our (Western) historically grown overarching form of sensibility (Bonnett, 2004). Without the notion of an underlying reality that is in some sense pre-given and autonomous, such sensibility would collapse, for it is premised on our relating to what is in some sense 'other'. This is reflected in, for example, the logic of such foundational ideas as 'knowledge', 'truth', 'reality', 'description'. Hence, while primordial ideas of nature and a natural order are indeed socially produced, they are not thereby purely arbitrary or optional, and within experience they occur as precisely *not* socially constructed. Today there may hardly be an animal, plant or landscape that has not been affected by, or does not bear the imprint of, human activity, but there always remains a dimension of their existence that is taken as not humanly authored. There is always something transcendent, that is beyond human activity (including sense-making), with which it engages.[2] For example, perhaps I look up at the clouds and suddenly the sun breaks through. Clearly the intelligibility of this occurrence is articulated through concepts of 'sun', 'clouds' and so forth, but *that* the sun breaks through at this moment is quite independent of those concepts and any facet of human intentionality. And how we treat nature, especially those elements of it that cannot 'answer back' can say a good deal about our moral stance.

While some further elaboration of the above is germane, for the moment it will be useful to adjust the focus on to the significance of speaking of us having a *place* in nature. Of course this can be conceived in an abstract way, in which humankind is formally located in some greater scheme of things—as it were, allocated its place in the cosmos. An example of this would be the hierarchical 'Great Chain of Being' originally conceived in antiquity and still prominent in the eighteenth century, and in which all things are ordered according to their 'degree of perfection', but where each is essential to the existence of the whole. Another would be a Darwinian 'Tree of Life' that expressed our evolutionary roots. Other modernist scientifically orientated conceptions include those of a blind causal system governed by the laws of physics; a realm of nested ecosystems; a vast cybernetic feedback system. (For a highly influential account of the latter, see Bateson, 1972.) The appropriateness or otherwise of such conceptions is a matter of ongoing debate, but certainly such ideas of our place in nature can (and did) have profound implications for how we conceive of ourselves and how we should behave. However, for present purposes I would like to explore a different way of approaching the topic by sketching a less discursive idea of what it is to be emplaced and its significance for morality.

I will argue that there are insights to be gained from conceiving our place in nature primarily not intellectually in terms of our location in some great abstract system such as those alluded to above, but rather in terms of our felt sense of place—and potentially of nature's presence—in the intimacy of our being in the particular locales that constitute the life-world of our daily existence; that is to say the places where concretely we *live* and in relationship with one another. I will argue not that conceptions of some all-encompassing greater whole are unimportant, but that they are best approached and understood through the portal of a heightened sense of such primary emplacements. I begin, then, with some brief observations on their character.

The anticipatory and ecstatic nature of emplacement[3]

It seems clear that it is not simply a contingent matter that our sense of our own existence is conditioned by our sense of where we are. In everyday experience, nothing occurs unplaced. We experience ourselves as always already in a world and this world is not one of some even spatio-temporal space governed by universal abstract laws, but one of distinct neighbourhoods characterised by changing local ambiences, events and significances. Elsewhere (Bonnett, 2009a), I have recounted how we are always (if often largely implicitly) to some degree claimed by the neighbourhoods in which we find ourselves. Our workplace, the place of a seminal encounter or tragic occurrence, can elicit sets of feelings and perceptions that incisively determine aspects of how and who we are when we are present there.

Relationships of *mutual anticipation*[4] between self and its environment that are both bodied and cerebral are in play here and to illustrate this I take the (rather extreme) example of someone who is forcibly removed from their most primordial neighbourhood: their home. Extracted from participation in the intimately woven fabric of people, artefacts, vistas and ambiences, routines, associations, aspirations and imaginings that hitherto have constituted their daily life, they can no longer be as once they were. The flow of immediate (and often minute) involvements that sustained them—for example, the familiar furniture and utensils that anticipated, and frequently invited, their thoughts and actions, such as the dishes by the sink that wait to be washed—has been broken.

Overall, there is an important general sense in which one *is* in one's dealings with a world: a milieu of prompts and claims that occur in particular places and that are always partly familiar, but also always taken as partly 'other', for even the most familiar thing is capable on occasion of coming to reveal a mysterious aspect or behave in an unexpected way. In this interplay of mutual anticipation self and world arise—as it were, each is called forth—and while such anticipation is frequently expressed through daily routines, it is not itself merely mechanical. Rather, it is always a form of standing outside oneself—*ecstasis*—of which at times it is possible to be strongly conscious as, say, with the sense of anticipation experienced when the walker sets off on a fine spring morning, open to the unknown that is to come—the sights, the smells, the textures, the ambiences and surprises, of say, different places and times of day. The keen attentiveness of which this speaks quickens life, gives a heightened sense of being. We are enlivened by this capacity to be beyond ourselves that enables felt encounters with what is other.

Anticipation in this sense occurs at many levels and, often less consciously salient, is involved in all that we do: the walker that the earth will bear her up, that the muddy patch ahead and the low overhanging bough will elicit adjustment to her stride, just as it might be quickened by anticipation of the view to be enjoyed when the brow of the hill is reached. Such anticipation is enacted implicitly through the very movements of the limbs and more generally it lies at the heart of the constant delicate, intelligent, adjustments both bodied and cerebral that we make within our proximate environment and through which we inhere in it—feeling in varying degree either 'at home' or discomforted (Bonnett, 2009a). Perhaps, unreflectively, we sink relaxed into a familiar armchair or lower ourselves stiffly into the solidity of an oak pew.

Now it is important to note here both that implicitly, at least, such being in a place always possesses a natural dimension and that awareness of this natural dimension, because of its independence from human intention, has a particular potential for taking us beyond ourselves, which itself is a requirement for moral relationships.

To begin with, the places in which we find ourselves are always at least in part constituted by the physical things that are present and although physical things are never purely physical, for they are always encountered in a matrix of human significances, they are experienced as having a brute dimension, a certain 'give-ness'. This is true in two senses: first, they can befall us as already present such that we can (in the Biblical sense, as it were) *behold* them, as, say, when we look up at the moon, or come across a beech tree in spring; second, the way in which they condition the space that they occupy. The presence of the river overhung by willows gives one place a certain ambience, as the chrome and glass table does another. In their reciprocal relationship with whatever else is present such things sustain a locale, each with its own particular quality of space, atmosphere.

Equally, in many ways each thing present—the way in which it is present, or 'presences' at any moment—draws upon its neighbourhood. There is an important sense in which a tree removed from the copse in which it sprang up and transplanted, say, to a shopping mall, is no longer the same tree. Bereft of its former neighbourhood, it can no longer presence quite as once it did. The bustle of wildlife that once inhabited or flitted through its canopy, the quiet moss that once covered its roots, the fall of its shadow at dusk on the particular plants and fallen boughs that populated its environs have all gone. Instead of a gentle sheltering presence it has become a silhouette on neon. Here, then, we have a limitation upon the extent to which any physical entity can be considered to exist autonomously, but equally in its sheer physicality it exists beyond human will—has a life of its own, displays a natural aspect—and unlike the contents of a computer screen, is most fully apprehended when all the senses are engaged and we become alive bodily as well as cognitively.

At this point I should make it clear that the view of nature that I am offering is not exclusively to be conceived in terms of a world of 'pure' entities in the sense of them being entirely innocent of human effects. Indeed, it is probably now true to say that with the global consequences of human activity there is no pure wilderness left, and that, as previously noted, often we find ourselves experiencing nature in the context of landscapes that clearly bear the imprint of the human hand. What, fundamentally, I have in mind when I speak of nature is not primarily some set of pristine entities, but *a dimension of experience* that to greater or lesser degree is present (if sometimes at several removes or, indeed, as withdrawn) in all perception. And key to this dimension of experience is an apprehension of that quality of the *self-arising* in things, previously mentioned—those aspects of things that are rightly experienced as essentially non-artefactual, ever beyond human authorship; present from out of themselves.

Hence, there is a distinction to be drawn between the 'thing *in* itself' conceived as what is beyond perception, incapable of being experienced at all (as with Kant) and the 'thing itself' as what has its own existence that might or might not be experienced, and in a variety of degrees and ways. The key point with the latter is that its primary being exceeds what is directly given in experience and yet exists as more than a mere logical inference: rather, it exists by virtue of an intuition of its—this thing's—alterity, the felt presence of what is withdrawn. For example, there are the many profiles currently hidden, the facets that lie sleeping within (such as the figuring of grain lying within a piece of timber), an incompletely known past and an anticipation of what is not yet. In this sense meaning is not determined by things, but neither is its relationship with them arbitrary. Meaning is not simply a subjective layer projected on brute reality, having no internal connection or reference to that reality and therefore no special validity—as if it all comes from us, is fully authored, sired, by us. The so-called 'external world' is not a Cartesian inference or a hypothesis, but what is closest to us; phenomenologically, we are embedded in it and it lies within us.

This sense of the alterity of natural things in their sheer standing there out of what is withdrawn means that they are inherently mysterious and hence an infinite source of mental and spiritual enrichment. This is one sense in which they exhibit intrinsic value. And while on this view it is quite proper to speak of some entities as being more natural than others or as natural in differing respects, rarely, if ever, do they possess no natural aspect or connection whatsoever. If the tree described above once clearly reposed in an environment in which nature as the self-arising resonated strongly and is diminished as a natural thing when it is removed from this, ultimately even a piece of computer code functioning electronically is intelligible in part, and perhaps at several removes, only by reference to phenomena (such as electricity) whose elemental existence is understood as not simply a product of human ingenuity or will. To say this is neither to imply that nature as the self-arising is apparent in all experience nor that 'literally' every phenomenon displays a natural aspect. Rather it is to reaffirm the point that a grounding intuition of nature as the self-arising is deeply embedded in our overarching form of sensibility, by reference to which everything that we encounter has its being, and is implicitly understood. Hence there is a level at which our sensibility is tacitly attuned to nature, and our emplaced experiences attest to this.

However, as I have acknowledged elsewhere (Bonnett, 2009b), none of this is to deny that some environments provide stronger invitations than others to apprehend any natural aspect and that the natural dimension can be very tenuous indeed in the places inhabited by some individuals. Perhaps for some city-dwellers it seems far-fetched to suppose that it could be otherwise. Their environment might be described as one of relentless artificiality, from the tarmac underfoot to the obliteration of the presence of the night sky by light and sound pollution, and to the diminution of the seasons and other natural rhythms—perhaps, even those of night and day—through other human interventions or dominant social habits. In such circumstances it may appear otiose to think of their emplacement as in any meaningful sense a portal to an appreciation of the self-arising. It is not, of course, that nature has no presence at all—rain or snow still fall, the granite kerbstones still have their own solidity, water still trickles, collects in puddles and reflects light in myriad ways, small-scale 'wild-life' may still be found under some stone or growing in some crevice—but it attracts little attention and has become invisible. Concern lies elsewhere. Yet a natural dimension remains, even if it is only experienced bodily as we trudge up some hill or shade our eyes, and in the concrete and glass still it remains possible to discern echoes of a more primitive give-ness. However nature is to be encountered, ultimately this only occurs authentically through the immediate and sensuous engagement with the particularity and manifold suchness of emplaced things rather than through abstraction and intellectually constructed models. For only in such places as sites of a blending of the physical and the cultural/social (understood now as arising aspects in relationship rather than independent pre-existing phenomena) can a substantive awareness of the autochthony of participatory self-arising occur.

And with regard to understanding our place in nature, to experience this is important for it is to experience the transcendent in the immanent and thereby to enter into an ecstatic relationship that has the potential to transport one to the horizon and beyond. Such ecstasis is the conduit for engagement with elemental powers that hold sway in the cosmos and that call for certain responses, hence connecting us in a primordial way with that cosmos. I have in mind here powers such as those of birth and death, growth and decay, lightening and darkening, sound and silence, motion and stillness that enliven our existence just as surely as anything that commerce or science can offer, even though these latter frequently tranquillise our awareness of them. It is through our participation in such powers that we are held in the world most authentically; they can light up our consciousness by making a silent call upon us that takes us into an infinitely extending and mysterious universe where the known constantly rubs shoulders with the ineffable.

Nature, place and normativity

It is our ability to live beyond ourselves, *with* the things of which we are conscious, that enables both the reflexivity necessary for self-awareness and the sensing of our emplacement in a world—a world of infinitely extended and interconnected significances made manifest to us through the presencing of things. A world of things sensed as proceeding on their own ineffable way, and whose sheer existence is essentially mysterious. It is as little possible for thought fully to encompass the being of a harebell silently emerging through the grass underfoot as it is for it fully to encompass the being of the Orion Nebula. Such being with things and the myriad demands that it places upon us is what it means to be in the world. Conceived in this way, places are imbued with feeling and value; they are inherently normative in the sense of offering intimations of possibilities of right conduct. These are expressed in the ways of proceeding that they invite, the attentions that they demand, the responsibilities that they offer and the mysteries that they intimate. While clearly this is true for a domestic place such as a dining room or kitchen, infused as they are with human intention, it is equally true for 'natural' places.

When we enter a wood or look out across a valley, we can be met by a host of possibilities of thought and action. These possibilities and their fittingness arise in the very occurrence of apprehending what is there. A natural place is shot through with intimations of fitting description and response. Unless a special story is told, a leaping salmon can no more be described as indolent than can a lover's touch be assumed uncaring. Simone Weil (2005, p. 234) once observed: 'To know that this man who is hungry and thirsty really exists as much as I do—that is enough, the rest follows of itself' (which is not to deny that considerations additional to those vouchsafed in this way might also become relevant). Similarly, to come across a young sapling gratuitously vandalised or an ancient oak carelessly bulldozed can bring a sense of outrage. In such cases values are not mere subjective additions to—projections upon—things: such things occur *with* their value, though not necessarily 'worn on the sleeve', rather sometimes waiting to be discerned. And awareness of nature in its quintessential alterity provides a particularly powerful experience of the mysterious other and its ability to gift inspiration and display intrinsic value that waits to be celebrated. Through the abstraction and systematisation involved in the construction of general explanations, scientific causal accounts necessarily efface this native occurring of things.

The foundation of such normativity, such intrinsic value, in nature is a matter of debate. (See, for example: Bonnett, 2004; Cooper, 1998; Elliot, 1997; Grange, 1997; Postma, 2006.) Whether ultimately it is anthropogenic and to be elucidated in terms of the aesthetic or the moral, or something more primitive, the point being made here is that the care and respect experienced is entirely fitting for an epistemic attitude that acknowledges the autonomy and mystery of nature. With this comes a certain tacit sense of nature's integrity, and the disruption of its 'rightness' can become explicit as, say, when we round a bend on a country path or enter a woodland dell to find it strewn with the remnants of fly tipping. Although the alterity of nature must qualify this sense of integrity, it remains the case that our sense of the health and indeed fulfilment of natural entities can be a powerful consideration in judging right action. Take the case of our own bodies. In relation to our physical health, ultimately we have to work with powers and processes beyond our authorship and while, no doubt, some aspects of 'good health' are socially constructed, fundamentally what counts as being healthy is in part at least determined by an organism's own internal—'natural'—ways. Heart failure could no more be a criterion of good health for us than canker could be for an apple tree. While always there might be overriding considerations, this sense of integrity, health and a being to fulfil that openness to things themselves supplies can provide strong normative measures in experience, particularly when it is strongly grounded, i.e. emplaced. Once awareness of such measures has occurred, it seems perverse simply to ignore them. They have become part of the moral life.

Of course, if this claim is accepted, it is still an open question as to what would count as a fitting response to such normative demands. Also, it might be argued that a person could (and some do) lead a fulfilled life without this kind of sensitivity—perhaps they are immersed in a rich social life in which intimations of the natural world are insignificant. In response to the first of these questions, it must readily be accepted that there can be no answer that is both specific and generalisable—just as with the question as to what would count as respecting a person on a particular occasion. In each case a specific response would arise from some intuition of the particular character of the emplaced individual concerned and sometimes this might require contemplation of a pretty high order. At base, the aspiration is not to produce some sort of moral code, rather it is to elucidate one of the *pre-conditions* of a properly informed ethical response (namely, a sensitivity to the presence and transcendent character of a natural dimension to the places in which we live). On the other hand, that such an idea of respectful response to aspects of nature is not merely fanciful is demonstrated by some stark examples of what clearly would *not* count, such as caging wild bears and inserting crude steel catheters into their gall bladders in order to extract fluid for the purpose of making an aphrodisiac (reported in *International Fund for Animal Welfare Newsletter*, January 2002). In response to the second question, in the final analysis the claim probably has to be conceded (although equally the potential for personal enrichment that nature offers to those who become engaged with it must also be granted). But this is already to adopt an anthropocentric stance and is to miss the central argument, which is that if things in nature possess intrinsic value, if this is indeed a feature of the world in which we live, right conduct requires an acknowledgement of this; it must be informed by consideration of its effects on natural things for their own sake. This becomes a morally relevant dimension of existence. No doubt it is this sensing of nature's integrity that accounts for that notion of the natural as wholesome that is still present within our general form of sensibility.

Hence emplacement in an environment where nature is either immediately salient or is allowed to reveal itself involves a form of attunement that is normative in the sense of responding to what is already present and underway: a dimension of being that is potential yet to be fulfilled and that therefore requires a certain participative letting be on our part. This will involve both emotion and will. It is not through grand idealisations that our place in nature primarily is given to us, rather through the minutia of manifold intimate involvements we receive the norms that imbue places and learn of the powers holding sway in the world. In this way we sense our active place within the world, learning how to receive what is gifted and gift what is received. In its celebration of alterity, clearly this speaks of a mode of caring that is open to non-anthropocentric impulses and a morality enacted not through the application of abstract principles, but through fitting response to what is arising in its sheer existential autonomy, embracing the ever-changing cadences of the populated (but not simply peopled) places in which always we find ourselves. The metaphysics of mastery runs out of space in the places where the intrinsic value of the non-human shines through.

Moral education

In contrast to one still highly influential characterisation of morality as 'a set of principles to govern human life in general' (Barrow, 2007, p. 28), it follows from an account of the kind developed above that fundamentally ethical concern does not arise in some pure form of the kind that can adequately be articulated in sets of universal abstract principles. Rather it is the case that our antecedent involvement in a place (and therefore the world) conditions all understanding, including the ethical. To note this is not necessarily to advocate the particularism of Dancy (2004), but it is to recognise the extent to which moral life is concerned with such and such an issue in such and such a context, and some aspects of the *participatory* nature of that context. Hence there is an intimate reciprocity between ethical and environmental concern that fundamentally initiates the character of our caring.

Some aspects of this have been recognised in recent ethical debate. For example, elucidating an idea introduced by Simon Blackburn (2001), Graham Haydon (2006) has explored the significance of the 'ethical environment'—the surrounding climate of ideas about how to live—for understanding moral action. In his account of how this contextualises and often implicitly informs an individual's actions there is a nod towards acknowledging both the significance of what I have termed the 'metaphysical climate' and potentially non-rational elements of moral judgement. However, he does not offer any focus upon the implicit anthropocentrism that lies at the heart of this ethical environment, as this article seeks to do. Yet anthropocentrism is revealed, for example, where he elucidates the standards for evaluating the ethical environment in terms of one that is healthy for and inclusive of the (rational) persons that inhabit it. Nor does he recognise the *moral* weight of non-rational aspects.

Similarly, an indication of current mainstream thinking in moral education is provided by Mark Halstead's recent survey of philosophical work in moral and citizenship education that records the current debates between a still influential liberal, rational morality and re-emerging alternative perspectives such as virtue and care ethics, without making reference to any idea of intrinsic value attaching to the natural environment and its moral significance (Halstead, 2010). The same is true of a discussion of the evolution of moral education given by Nel Noddings and Michael Slote (2003).

Perhaps the most fundamental point for moral education that arises from the account developed in this article is that it needs to be understood as essentially a poetic and holistic endeavour that entails a metaphysical re-orientation. While rational principles have a part to play, their interpretation is subordinate to a poetic apprehension of people in their felt environments (i.e. as emplaced) that have both local and transcendent dimensions, and in which all—not only human—participants are capable of possessing or disclosing intrinsic value.

Such a position can be articulated in a number of ways. For example, in a recent collection that discusses the significance of aspects of 'green' thought for education and culture, Heesoon Bai (2009) speaks of a certain 'psychic numbing' that currently pervades our outlook on the world and of the need to re-animate the essentially disembodied perception that she argues was set in train by the views of Plato and Descartes, and that undermined the worth and validity of a more empathic participatory consciousness as a way of knowing and relating to the world. This need to change not simply the content of, but the very modality of our perception is echoed in Bob Jickling's paper (2009) in the same volume. There he discusses ways in which the ascendence of the desire for control has impoverished learning in educational institutions and how there is a need to rehabilitate emotional understanding into educational thinking and to reaffirm the experiential, the sensuous, the particular: an ontological attentiveness that re-enables students to be 'pierced' by the *thisness* of the things that they encounter. This is a learning that cannot be pre-specified and closely measured, rather it is a 'happy learning that just announces itself' (Jickling, 2009).[5]

Here we have strong resonances with Dewey's ideas of genuine experience involving an 'undergoing' (Dewey, 1934) and Simone Weil's description of attention as consisting of 'suspending our thought, leaving it detached, empty and ready to be penetrated by the object …' (Weil, 1977, p. 56). Something of the potential of such a relationship with things for practical life in general, and a suggestion that it need not involve unduly mystical elements, is nicely illustrated in an account of attentiveness given by Richard Smith (1998). And certainly, intense attention to the things and activities of everyday life and to attempting to articulate (always inadequately) our multi-layered lived relationships with the non-human (animate and inanimate) that conditions our existence through word (struggling for *le mot juste*), art and music is necessary to a moral education that seeks to be properly grounded. By this means new metaphors can arise that provide opportunities for deepened perception and engagement.

A general point here is that insofar as moral education incorporates notions of moral thinking or moral knowledge that draw upon broader conventional ideas of knowledge such as rationalism (for example, when it seeks to develop moral reasoning of a Kantian kind as with Kohlberg), any radical reappraisal of currently dominant epistemologies has significant implications for it. On the account presented here moral education will require a critical examination of modernist humanism and the scientism that is its legacy so as to reveal the exploitative nature of modern reason, including its silences and the kinds of ignorance that it relies on to sustain its anthropocentrism. Lack of care for and disrespect of nature has the same root as these attitudes when they are exhibited towards persons: the metaphysics of mastery. It follows that moral education will have a direct interest in pedagogical strategies for disturbing and making strange both everyday and 'official' consciousness so as to create space for the imagining, development, or retrieval of alternative more respectful cultural spaces and places, and the possibility of enactment of the normative measures that arise. Such practice could include, for example, spending time in out of classroom places in which self-arising nature is a powerful presence, experiencing the knowledges of different cultures and their relationships to nature and places, gaining a diversity of natural history knowledge, engaging with discomfiting testimonial literature that provokes us to consider the 'difficult knowledge' of our implicatedness in ecological issues (McKenzie, 2008), adopting some aspect of the local environment such as a stream or stretch of unused land, integrating nature into the school campus. A moral education that recognises the need to challenge the current dominant Western metaphysical climate that is rapidly becoming global cannot duck the difficult challenge of attempting to create opportunities to reveal it and to dislodge it where it can.

Of course, the views of Bai and Jickling described above might be considered to be hopelessly nostalgic returns to primitivism or romanticism. That they are returns to earlier, now frequently disparaged, ways of seeing the world is certainly true. But whether this is a reason for rejecting them is far from self-evident and remains an important open question that has extensive implications for moral education. At the very least we might consider whether we need to rehabilitate aspects of Romanticism into our thinking about morality and moral education. While the notion that we can acquire moral precepts from nature in any straightforward way as suggested in Baron d'Holbach's *Systême de la nature* of 1780, or indeed later and more subtly by Wordsworth and Coleridge,[6] is problematic, the supreme importance that the Romantics attached to the imagination as a participatory and unifying power that can substantiate and vivify reason by facilitating entry into the environment and some sort of communion with the life and spirit of nature is surely worthy of consideration. This is one way in which possibilities of alternative ways of being—living in different places—to those sustained by the status quo can be opened up.

If, as previously argued, we spend our lives in a world of places in which nature is a key—if sometimes highly tacit—constituent, to understand this world and its moral demands requires ways of knowing it that allow it to show itself in all its facets. And this is not simply a matter of intellectual re-orientation, but concerns the character of our being. That is to say it is ontological as well as epistemological. It reaffirms the importance to education of embodied awareness, being in amongst things, participative (as against purely instrumental) activity, rather than looking on, the spectatorial, analytical gaze (see, for example, Hung, 2008). It affirms knowledge by acquaintance in which all the senses are in play and yet in which a contemplative spirit holds sway.[7] Such a position invites exploration of an idea of moral education that premises the idea of moral agency on that of poetic receptiveness. In doing this it intimates an enlarged sense of moral agency: one that is less exclusively pre-occupied with the model of an autonomous rational agent and that seeks to sensitise us to possibilities of an enabling passivity on our part that properly recognises the play of non-human agency (whose intentional character, if any, we might suppose will be quite different to that of human agency) and the ways in which there is a reciprocal co-responsibility for the character of the places in which we live. Clearly, this represents a radical challenge to the traditional ethical position of conceiving moral obligation within a social contract that can only hold between rational agents.

The argument that moral education should include attention to a relationship with nature as a relationship with what is in a significant sense both emplaced and transcendent raises some further important considerations. In alerting us to the significance of alterity in the world, it suggests a counterbalance to practices that draw upon other influential bases for moral education such as communitarianism, care ethics, and virtue ethics. With regard to the first, while an emphasis on place resonates strongly with communitarianism, the themes of ecstasis and transcendence add poignancy to reservations about too exclusive an emphasis on initiation into a local moral culture. With regard to the second, while it shares with care ethicists a recognition of the centrality to morality of concrete relationships, the assumptions of underlying commonality with the cared for made by care ethicists could be seen as interposing a filter that endangers a more direct connection with them in their otherness. From the perspective of transcendence, ecstasis as an open ability to stand beyond ourselves rather than empathy or sympathy is what is most fundamental to being moral—allowing the other to be itself rather than presuming to know in advance—to comprehend—its feelings and purposes, and indeed whether or not it has feelings and purposes.[8] On this view, it is not so much that on occasion, rightly, our actions might be informed by a sense of what someone else could be feeling, it is that we need to be alert to the ever-present danger of responses that express *our* expectations prescribing their sense of what *they* should be feeling. Intimately emplaced life is too subtle and many-faceted for this to express true moral regard.

With regard to virtue ethics, while such a genuinely receptive-responsive capacity is a virtue to be cultivated, its grounding and character is different to pure virtue ethics in the sense that it is understood as not simply as good in itself and for what it reveals about the inner life of the agent who possesses it. It is these things, but it is a virtue because it is called forth as a fitting response to the transcendent other. Iris Murdoch expressed something of this and the synergies it implies between moral education and education more broadly when she wrote:

> Art and morals are, with certain provisos ... one. Their essence is the same. The essence of both of them is love. Love is the extremely difficult realisation that something other than oneself is real. Love, and so art and morals, is the discovery of reality. (Murdoch, 1959, p. 51)

Insofar as attention to our place in nature—in addition to inviting us to re-conceive the community of bearers of moral value and the nature of moral obligation—cues us to a dimension of being that both is essential to developing a proper moral regard for the non-human and is provocative in thinking about what counts as proper moral regard for the human, it surely has considerable significance for our understanding of moral education. The notion of emplaced transcendence that it foregrounds offers an enriched terrain for the development of moral sensibility and practice.

Notes

1. Throughout this article 'metaphysics', 'metaphysical setting', 'metaphysical climate' are understood as referring to those deep motives holding sway within a culture at a particular time and that by shaping our perceptions of, and ways of relating to, the world install us in a particular version of reality. 'Metaphysics of mastery' refers to the growing ascendency in modern Western rationality of instrumental motives and the will to power that ultimately produces a reality in which everything is turned into a resource, their meaning and value becoming a function of how they show up in utilitarian calculations (see Bonnett, 2000).
2. It should be noted that on this view while a distinction is drawn between what is experienced as human and what is experienced as nature, this does not make the view dualistic in the sense of supposing that nature is authentically understood as an object for an independent subjectivity, denying that we exist *in* nature, or that consciousness is in an important sense part of nature. It simply asserts that human consciousness (or its equivalent) is of a special character: it is the place in which things show up—are encountered, are understood, become intelligible—*as* things (mysterious and inhering in a world). As will be clear from the arguments developed in this article, consciousness so conceived is regarded as being intimately bound in with a world of things and places (in which our relationship with nature is pivotal)—to the extent that it is nothing without them.
3. While some aspects of the account that follows are in part inspired by the seminal treatment of these ideas by Martin Heidegger (1962) in *Being and time*, it does not pretend to be an exegesis of Heidegger's thinking and, indeed, in some respects it might be seen as nuancing matters rather differently.
4. The term 'anticipation' is preferred in this context to, say, 'significance' or 'expectation' because the latter can denote an experience that is too exclusively cerebral, abstract and explicitly stateable. 'Anticipation' is interpreted as a more fluid occurrence—one of, as it were, an 'understanding in motion' (see Bonnett, 2009a).
5. This is not, of course, to deny that sometimes it might occur on the back of a prolonged struggle to understand.
6. See, for example Wordsworth's *The tables turned* (1798), *Lines composed a few miles above Tintern Abbey* (1798), *Ode: intimations of mortality* (1807) (Wordsworth, 1994 edn.).
7. I use the term 'knowledge' here in a sense that does not imply totalising comprehension, but rather an awareness of intimations of potentiality. Hence the epistemic stance that emerges in this article is precisely one that eschews any aspiration of possessive grasping in favour of one that seeks the knowing of open receptivity, and acknowledges, in the context of the current metaphysical climate, the preparation of heart and mind that is frequently necessary to achieve a way of acting in the world in which such receptivity can occur.
8. I refer here to that sense of empathy that presumes an ability to 'put oneself in the shoes' of another, to know 'just how you are feeling'. Here the other is turned into an object of (totalising) knowledge and the expression of empathy can express a power relationship in which the empathiser (often despite their intentions) sets themselves up to legitimate the feelings of the other. All empathy and sympathy assume a level of commonality, and this assumption can be misplaced.

References

Bai, H. (2009). Reanimating the universe: environmental education and philosophical animism. In M. McKenzie, P. Hart, H. Bai, & B. Jickling (Eds.), *Fields of green. Restorying culture, environment, and education*. Cresskill, NJ: Hampton Press.

Barrow, R. (2007). *An introduction to moral philosophy and moral education*. Oxford: Routledge.

Bateson, G. (1972). *Steps to an ecology of mind*. Chicago, IL: University of Chicago Press.

Blackburn, S. (2001). *Being good: A short introduction to ethics*. Oxford: Oxford University Press.

Bonnett, M. (2000). Environmental concern and the metaphysics of education. *Journal of Philosophy of Education, 34*(4), 591–602.

Bonnett, M. (2004). *Retrieving nature: Education for a post-Humanist age*. Oxford: Blackwell.

Bonnett, M. (2009a). Schools as places of unselving: an educational pathology? In G. Dall'Alba (Ed.), *Exploring education through phenomenology. Diverse approaches*. Oxford: Wiley-Blackwell.

Bonnett, M. (2009b). Systemic wisdom, the 'selving' of nature, and knowledge transformation: education for the 'greater whole'. *Studies in Philosophy and Education: Environmental Concern and the Transformation of Knowledge,* (special issue) 28(1), 39–49.

Butt, J. (1963). *The poems of Alexander Pope*. London: Methuen.

Cooper, D. (1998). Aestheticism and environmentalism. In D. Cooper & J. Palmer (Eds.), *Spirit of the environment*. London: Routledge.

Dancy, J. (2004). *Ethics without principles*. Oxford: Oxford University Press.

Dewey, J. (1934). *Art as experience*. New York, NY: Minton, Balch and Company.

Elliot, R. (1997). *Faking nature*. London: Routledge.

Grange, J. (1997). *Nature. An environmental cosmology*. New York, NY: State University of New York Press.

Halstead, J.M. (2010). Moral and citizenship education. In R. Bailey, R. Barrow, D. Carr, & C. McCarthy (Eds.), *The SAGE handbook of philosophy of education*. London: SAGE.

Haraway, D. (1991). *Simians, cyborgs and women: The reinvention of nature*. London: Free Association Books.

Haydon, G. (2006). *Education, philosophy and the ethical environment*. London: Routledge.

Heidegger, M. (1962). *Being and time*. Oxford: Blackwell.

Heidegger, M. (1977). *The question concerning technology and other essays*. New York, NY: Harper Row.

Holbach, Baron d' (1780). *Système de la nature*. London.

Hung, R. (2008). Education for and through nature: A Merleau-Pontian approach. *Studies in Philosophy and Education, 27*(5), 355–367.

Jickling, B. (2009). Sitting on an old grey stone. Meditations on emotional understanding. In M. McKenzie, P. Hart, H. Bai, & B. Jickling (Eds.), *Fields of green. Restorying culture, environment, and education*. Cresskill, NJ: Hampton Press.

Marshall, P. (1995). *Nature's web*. London: Cassell.

McKenzie, M. (2008). The places of pedagogy: Or, what we can do with culture through intersubjective experiences. *Environmental Education Research, 14*(3), 361–373.

Murdoch, I. (1959). The sublime and the good. *Chicago Review, 13*(3), 42–45.

Noddings, N., & Slote, M. (2003). Changing notions of the moral and of moral education. In N. Blake, P. Smeyers, R. Smith, & P. Standish (Eds.), *The Blackwell guide to the philosophy of education*. Oxford: Blackwell.

Postma, D.W. (2006). *Why care for nature? In search of an ethical framework for environmental responsibility and education*. Dordrecht: Springer.

Smith, R.D. (1998). Spirit of middle earth: practical thinking for an instrumental age. In D. Cooper & J. Palmer (Eds.), *Spirit of the environment*. London: Routledge.

Soper, K. (1995). *What is nature?*. Oxford: Blackwell.

Weil, S. (1977). *Waiting on God*. London: Routledge & Kegan Paul.

Weil, S. (2005). *Simone Weil: An anthology*. London: Penguin Books.

Wordsworth, W. (1994 edn.). *The collected poems of William Wordsworth*. Ware, Herts: Wordsworth Editions.

Questioning the idea of the individual as an autonomous moral agent

C.A. Bowers
University of Oregon, USA

This paper examines ways in which current moral values are influenced by earlier patterns of thinking carried forward in root metaphors whose meanings were often framed by the analogues settled upon in the past by thinkers who were influenced by the silences and prejudices of their culture. It is argued that such tacitly inherited metaphors reproduce the myth of the individual as a moral agent and that this both is ecologically unsustainable and undermines other important ways of understanding the individual. In various ways the form of critical thinking to which it gives rise stands in the way of individuals exercising what Gregory Bateson refers to as their 'ecological intelligence' in a manner that properly takes account of the interdependent nature of cultural and natural ecologies. It is argued that if in the West (at least) a shift could be made to relying on 'ecology' as the dominant root metaphor the whole system of Western moral values would undergo a radical change to one better suited to a current Western environmental situation.

Introduction

It is unfortunate that the ideas of Gregory Bateson have not been taken more seriously by educational reformers. In his two most important books, *Steps to an ecology of mind* (1972), and *Mind and nature* (1979), he introduces five key ideas that provide a conceptual framework for understanding why schools and universities continue to perpetuate the misconceptions of earlier times when there was no understanding of environmental limits. As I have written an entire book on the educational reform implications of these ideas I will only summarise them here (Bowers, 2011). They are: (1) 'recursive epistemologies', here understood as deep conceptual patterns that provide pervasive taken-for-granted interpretative frameworks and that are repeated tacitly over the centuries; (2) both cultural and natural ecosystems are sustained by the circulation of information which Bateson describes as 'the difference which makes a difference'; (3) 'the map is not the territory' in the sense that the metaphorical basis of our conceptual maps were constituted in the past by people who could not be aware of our current situations; (4) 'double bind' thinking occurs when what are taken to be progressive ideas actually undermine the possibility of a sustainable future; (5) 'Level III' thinking that involves learning to question the culture's deep taken-for-granted assumptions (or recursive epistemologies).

This brief summary may leave readers with the impression that ignoring Bateson's ideas has enabled them to avoid becoming mired in a series of abstractions. This would be an entirely wrong conclusion to reach, as Bateson's thinking reflects an ecological form of intelligence that recognises the patterns that connect within cultural and natural ecologies. In effect, his thinking challenges a number of misconceptions that continue to perpetuate the ideas that gave conceptual direction and moral legitimacy to the industrial/consumer-dependent culture that is now, in the name of progress, being globalised even though it is rapidly degrading the natural systems that all life depends upon. The misconception that will be the focus here is that the individual is an autonomous moral agent, and that she/he is also the autonomous source of ideas—especially when engaging in critical thinking. Indeed, the emphasis of educational reformers on promoting critical thinking, with some reformers such as Paulo Freire (1970) and Moacir Gadotti (2002) claiming that all forms of socialisation undermine individual autonomy, is one of the most prominent recursive conceptual and ethnocentric ways of thinking promoted by many educational reformers.

What needs to be clearly recognised is that both the idea of individual intelligence and, by extension, that the individual is an autonomous moral agent, are based on long-held misconceptions that have their roots in the mythopoetic narratives in the Bible, in democratic political traditions that now need to be conserved, in the abstract and ethnocentric traditions of Western philosophers, in the mindset reinforced by the industrial culture, and in the formal educational process where students are told to think for themselves and to choose their own values. The personal pronoun used in such statements as 'I think', 'I want' and 'I see' is a part of daily discourse that reinforces the idea of being an autonomous self-directing individual who makes subjective claims on the world. Of course there have been other influences on the current idea that there is such as entity as an autonomous, rationally self-directing moral agent. The introduction of perspective by early artists in the fifteenth century, political tracts that transformed the idea of the individual as a subject into that of a citizen, and the daily experiences of making choices in the market place and in cyberspace, have all reinforced the idea of individual autonomy. Given this summary, it might seem natural to suppose that the Western idea of the autonomous individual now celebrated by libertarian ideologues and market liberals (who are mistakenly referred to as conservatives) should now be promoted in the rest of the world's cultures.

It will be argued that there are three problems with the idea of the autonomous individual. The first is that it is based on historically rooted misconceptions. The second is that it is ecologically unsustainable. The third is that it does not take account of how individualism is understood in many cultures that have not yet been entirely colonised by the West. Indeed, if we are to learn how to live in ways that have a smaller ecological footprint, and that are less dependent upon the consumer lifestyle that previous generations took for granted (and is now disappearing as workers are being replaced by computers), it will be necessary to learn how to exercise *ecological* intelligence—which is profoundly different from the exercise of individual intelligence. Given the shortness of space, I will first explain the basis for making the argument that individually centred rational thought and moral judgement are an ecologically unsustainable myth. I will then provide a short explanation of the connections between ecological intelligence, the form of moral decision-making consistent with the exercise of ecological intelligence, and the educational reforms that promote ecological intelligence.

The linguistic roots of the misconception that moral values are individually chosen

As in most aspects of human thinking, including the thinking of people who are providing others with data, objective knowledge and theories that are supposedly free of cultural influences, we rely upon linguistic processes that go largely unrecognised. This is partly because so much of culture is taken for granted, including the languaging processes that influence what is taken to be 'reality'. The focus here will be on making explicit how an understanding of several characteristics of these languaging processes bring into question the widely held idea that the individual is an autonomous moral agent—and, by extension, that the critical reflection of the supposedly autonomous individual always leads to progressive change. But first it is necessary to identify the layers of misconceptions that underlie the goal of many educational reformers who are still in denial that there is an ecological crisis—and that the earlier traditions of thinking they take for granted are major contributors to exacerbating it.

First misconception

The dominant view of educators at all levels, and the one reinforced in print-based storage and communication, is that language is a conduit in a sender/receiver process of communication. This misconception is essential to sustaining the idea that individuals are original thinkers, and that objective data and information can be communicated to others. What this widely held misconceptions hides is that words, with the exceptions of prepositions and conjunctions, are metaphors. If we can avoid being taken in by the current arguments of George Lakoff and Mark Johnson that metaphors originate in embodied experiences that are then encoded in the neurons of the brain (Lakoff & Johnson, 1999), we can recognise that the words (metaphors) we learn from our language community have a history. These words (iconic metaphors) include 'individualism', 'technology', 'tradition', 'ecology', 'markets', 'progress', 'woman' and so forth—indeed, the entire vocabulary of the language community which will vary from culture to culture. The conduit view of language is dependent upon viewing words as referring to real things, to what is objectively known, and to representing rationally based ideas (that is, abstract ideas) as having a universal standing.

Second misconception

This lies in ignoring the fact that words, as metaphors, have a history. Awareness of this fact leads to a different understanding: namely, the meaning of words (metaphors) is framed by the analogues chosen in earlier times as a way of understanding what is new or what is being rethought in light of new experiences. Thus, in earlier times the analogues that framed the meaning of the word 'woman' were limited to perhaps four or five attributes, while today the number of attributes have been expanded to include being an artist, mathematician, engineer and so on. It was not too long ago that it was morally permissible to denigrate a woman if she showed too much intelligence or was too competitive. The analogues settled upon by Enlightenment thinkers for understanding the word 'tradition' included all the abuses of the feudal era, and the meaning of the word for most educators today includes these analogues—and not the non-monetised intergenerational knowledge, craft skills, and healing practices that were part of the cultural commons of that era. In not recognising the early framing of the meaning of the metaphors we rely upon today, which leads to thinking of them as representing an objective reality, educational reformers (as well as politicians and others—including philosophers and social theorists) ignore how the analogues settled upon in earlier times are encoded in the language used today—and how learning to think and communicate in the language of the culture carries forward the misconceptions and silences of earlier times, as well as the moral guidelines for how to respond to the different culturally prescribed attributes of plants, animals, and people. In some cultures, water is sacred, while in others water is to be treated as a commodity—and both perspectives involve moral behaviours that are deeply rooted in the respective culture's mythopoetic narratives. It is my argument that it is the lack of a deep understanding of the conceptual and moral foundations of the culture that leads the Western thinker to view moral choice as an expression of her/his autonomy.

There are two points that need to be emphasised here. The first is that so-called individual intelligence is influenced by the form of intelligence (including the ignorance and prejudices) that is encoded in the meaning of historically constituted metaphors that we have not reconstituted in terms of culturally and ecologically informed analogues. An example of reconstituting earlier analogues can be seen in how the word 'wilderness' was earlier associated with danger and a resource to be exploited, whereas today the analogues that environmentalists associate with the word is health and sustainability. With the dominant analogue that once framed how wilderness was understood, it was morally permissible to kill and destroy anything that was regarded as 'wild' (Snyder, 1990). The recursive epistemology, which I refer to as the root metaphors of a culture (Bowers, 2011), can be seen today in how so-called intelligent people think of organic processes in the same metaphorical language that Johannes Kepler and other scientists of the sixteenth century associated with machines and later with the industrial process. Other recursive patterns can be seen in thinking of change as a linear form of progress, of a human-centred world (which goes back to the Book of Genesis in the Bible), and in thinking that individual autonomy is a desired goal even though complete autonomy would require being emancipated from the influence of the languaging processes essential for communicating with others.

The metaphorical nature of language not only carries forward the insights, misconceptions and silences of earlier thinkers, it is also essential to communicating about how relationships are to be understood and acted upon. How relationships are understood is at the core of moral decisions. That is, the language of a culture intergenerationally passes along how the attributes of the participants in the relationships are to be understood. It is in the nature of these culturally prescribed attributes that we find the moral values that are learned at a taken-for-granted (that is non-reflective) level of awareness—in classrooms, in conversations with others, from the media and from institutional settings such as churches and work settings. Individuals may not question the attributes, such as thinking of weeds as having no value and thus to be dealt with a pesticide or doubting that a woman possesses the requisite attributes to be the pilot of a Boeing 777. Moral choices are often, as these two examples suggest, based on prejudices that are linguistically passed along through the process of primary socialisation. And prejudices are prime examples of moral choices that are encoded in the language of a cultural group—and thus are seldom an expression of an autonomous moral choice. To learn the language of one's culture is to learn the moral values associated with the culturally defined attributes. Further evidence that moral values are influenced by the analogues that frame the meaning of words in the vocabulary of different cultural groups can be seen in how different traditions in Judaism, Christianity, Islam and Buddhism lead to differences in moral choices. The moral values of each religion reflect how the attributes of the participants in different relationships are understood. Within a particular tradition of Christian thinking, it is morally permissible to ignore the plight of the poor and destitute as it is assumed that the individual lacks a work ethic and the drive to get ahead. If it were not for the ethnocentric thinking and lack of historical perspective of some educational reformers who make the claim that individual autonomy is essential to moral decision making, the influence of religions and the metaphorical language they privilege might be recognised.

Aside from the often unrecognised influence of religious traditions, and the mythopoetic narratives of different cultures, there are other examples of how moral choices and behaviours influenced by the analogues settled upon in the past continue to frame the meaning of words and thus the moral choices of supposedly autonomous individuals. The analogues that framed the meaning of such words as 'tradition', 'technology', 'data', 'progress', and so forth, continue to influence how many educators fail to help students understand the moral issues that need to be considered in relationship to how these words are used today. When the word 'tradition' is represented in the classroom in terms of the analogues of backwardness, obstacles to progress and the pre-rational and pre-scientific, there is less likelihood that students will consider what is being overturned by technological innovations and market forces. Awareness of the ecological crisis and the impact of technology on the workplace should lead to making moral decisions about which aspects of intergenerational knowledge that have a smaller ecological footprint and that enable people to be less dependent upon consumerism should be intergenerationally renewed. If students are left with the long-standing analogues that represent technology as both a neutral tool and as the expression of progress, they are not likely to recognise that there are moral decisions to be made about the destructive effects of different technologies—such as the loss of privacy, the displacement of workers and craft knowledge and the increased tendency toward abstract thinking that accompanies the educational uses of computers. The analogues that frame the meaning of 'progress' continue to be responsible for so little attention being given by educators to the moral issues associated with current examples of what is being represented as progress—and few so-called autonomous students are aware of these moral issues. Their silence is, in effect, a moral response. However, it is one that supports ecologically and politically problematic policies. These examples, which could be multiplied many times over, need to be understood as further evidence that ignoring the metaphorical nature of the language has moral consequences.

Individual choice and ecological intelligence in moral decision-making

By now, many readers may assume that I am denying that there is any such thing as an individual decision. This is definitely not the case. Each person has a biographically distinct life, but it is framed by the conceptual and moral boundaries that are largely influenced by the languaging processes of the culture into which she/he is born. To put this another way, the embodied experiences of the person are culturally mediated in ways that are seldom fully recognised. Some will question beliefs and practices that others take for granted—and this will represent a distinct quality of their way of giving individualised expression to their culturally mediated experiences. In the West, this behaviour tends to be viewed as the expression of an individually autonomous moral agent, but this tendency toward generalisation overlooks the areas of cultural silence where moral decisions should be made. In some cultures, such as in the West, decisions that challenge the moral orthodoxies of others are a moral matter and are rewarded by some segments of society, while in other cultures questioning the moral orthodoxies will be punished or censored by a collective silence.

The intentional nature of the consciousness of the biographically distinct individual means that individualised choices are continually being made—about friends, food, where one goes in cyberspace, what questions to raise in a class discussion, how to spend one's time (given certain constraints), and so forth. There are even individualised choices about political and spiritual matters. However, these choices are not entirely a matter of autonomous decision-making; rather they are circumscribed in most instances by the silences reflecting what the culture wants to repress and by what cannot be expressed given the limitations of the culture's language. These observations raise questions that few educational reformers, especially those in denial about the ecological crisis, want to consider as they promote the idea that one of the primary goals of education is to further emancipate the individual and to promote changes that are assumed to be progressive in nature.

This view of the purpose of education has become a widely held orthodoxy among progressive and social justice educational reformers. It is even the basis of thinking among the small group of reformers who are attempting to rehabilitate the legacy of Paulo Freire by representing him as an early environmental thinker. This group now goes by the label of 'ecopedagogy' (Kahn, 2010). What is important about the current way that critical inquiry is framed metaphorically is that the analogues represent progress and traditions in binary terms. That is, all traditions are to be questioned and reconstituted by the autonomous decisions of the students. It is important to note that this approach to critical inquiry seldom relies upon a grounded, ethnographically based examination of the traditions that are re-enacted in daily experience. Rather, it is based on the same abstract thinking that leads to assuming that change and transformation are inherently progressive in nature. This way of thinking overlooks the fact that it is ethnocentric, is based on the analogues that Enlightenment thinkers succeeded in associating with the word 'tradition', and ironically aligns with the view of tradition that technocrats and market-liberals want to promote in order to create greater dependency upon consumerism. That the technocrats and market liberals also want the autonomous individual to become the social norm is not understood by most educational reformers. The logic in the thinking of technocrats and market liberals should be plain to anyone who is aware that as the intergenerational traditions that support the largely non-monetised cultural commons are destroyed, the autonomous individual will be dependent upon the industrial/consumer lifestyle for meeting the most basic needs.

The other characteristic of critical inquiry that is seldom recognised relates to the way that every group in society, from religious fundamentalists, political extremists, to economic and social interest groups, relies upon the exercise of critical inquiry in working out their strategy for achieving the success of their political agenda. Here critical inquiry serves many ends, both useful and destructive. Within different cultures, it is exercised by different social groups, with many indigenous cultures making it the responsibility of the members who have demonstrated an ability to put self-interest aside in order to make decisions that benefit the current and future generations. This is profoundly different from the approach taken by Western educational reformers who want students who already exist (as I have argued) in a technologically induced state of cultural amnesia to make decisions about what to overturn in order to achieve greater autonomy and progress.

Given the ecological crisis, and the slippery political slope that could easily lead, given the current level of technological surveillance and the power of corporations, to a police state, a radically modified approach to critical inquiry is more needed than ever before. Simply stated, it should bring into focus the many traditions and political/economic agendas that are further exacerbating social injustices, the ecological crisis, and the colonisation of other cultures to a Western lifestyle (see, for example, Bowers, 2002). But its other purpose, which is equally important, is to identify the traditions of the diverse cultural and environmental commons that reduce dependency upon consumerism, and upon the technologies that further marginalise awareness of community patterns of mutual support and the changes occurring in the natural environment. The gains in social justice—which range from the labour movement, civil rights for different marginalised groups and legal protections gained through past struggles—are now part of the traditions that critical inquiry should help to protect. Some educational theorists, who like to reduce their agendas to evocative metaphors, suggest that critical inquiry and emancipation are essential to a 'transformative' and thus progressive future. What they overlook is that the scientific/technological/corporate alliance is the greatest transformative force today. Given that increasingly little is now regarded as morally prohibited from being incorporated into the market economy, it is necessary to adopt a more balanced view of critical inquiry—one that recognises the need to renew the intergenerational traditions that are less destructive of the natural environment, that foster the discovery of personal talents and skills, that strengthen the traditions of community self-sufficiency and mutual support and strengthen the students' experience of community.

Ironically, what is being suggested here is a radical approach to challenging the current alliance of scientific/technological/corporate culture that continues to emphasise economic growth that deskills and displaces the need for workers and further degrades the viability of natural systems in an era of exploding populations. One part of this radical approach to rethinking the conceptual and moral orthodoxies that align the agendas of progressive educational reformers with the industrial culture they criticise is the need to recognise the many ways in which the myth of individual intelligence is reinforced in classrooms—all the way through graduate school. If educational reformers were to take seriously Bateson's key insights about the recursive epistemologies that are reproduced across the curriculum (including at the university level), the connections between the language issues and double bind thinking, and the ways in which ecological intelligence is exercised when attention is given to the differences which make a difference in the cultural and natural ecologies (or what he refers to as the patterns that connect), they would then recognise the many ways in which ecological intelligence is exercised in daily life. As he points out in the example of swinging an axe, the previous swing of the axe leads to a change in the cut-face of the tree, and this difference makes a difference in the angle and force of the following stroke. Other examples of ecological intelligence include becoming aware of how the introduction of a toxic chemical makes a difference in whether a gene plays its traditional role in the ecology of a life-forming process, in performing in a game situation where the differences in the actions of others lead to a continual modification in one's own actions, in preparing a recipe where differences in heat and use of ingredients are carefully observed and adjusted for, in responding to the patterns of meta-communication of the Other, in thinking reflexively about what is taken for granted by others, and so forth. Ecological intelligence always involves responding to the differences occurring in our environment, including how the Other (ranging from the micro level of chemical processes, the macro-level climate changes, to the cultural level of behaviours and values) is always an integral part of the process. It is the opposite of the Cartesian view of intelligence, or the form of de-contextualised thinking that is reinforced by reliance upon the abstractions in print-based storage and communication (Ong, 1982).

In effect, the basic difference between individual and ecological intelligence is that the former too often relies upon abstract thinking, where responses are formulaic rather than based on awareness of the differences which make a difference in ongoing relationships and patterns. Ecological intelligence involves relying upon all the senses, awareness of ongoing changes in local contexts, awareness of the taken-for-granted assumptions of the culture, the consequences upon the actions of the other participants in the local cultural and natural ecologies. Ecological intelligence, in effect, takes account of relationships whereas individual intelligence is more conditioned to think of things, events and relationships in terms of isolated entities and in terms of linear casual relationships. Individual intelligence is also dependent upon ignoring that language has a history, is metaphorical, and that it leads to unconsciously relying upon past ways of thinking for understanding current situations. It also relies more on sight, which is increasingly focused on the computer monitor and the cell-phone screen, than the other senses.

Bateson provides a way of understanding moral behaviour within an ecologically informed world. He put it this way: '... in no system which shows mental characteristics can any part have unilateral control over the whole. In other words, the mental characteristics of the system are immanent, not in some part, but in the system as a whole' (1972, p. 316). He further notes that the unit of survival is not the individual, but the system as a whole. To summarise the moral principle that is central to the exercise of ecological intelligence: moral behaviour must always take into account how it affects the relationships within the larger cultural and natural ecology. It must also be in support of life-sustaining processes that will affect the prospects of future generations. Our lives are always embedded in relationships, including the ecologies of ideas and identities that need to be taken into account in making moral decisions.

If readers review what was previously written about the ethnocentric and abstract thinking that underlie the idea that the individual makes autonomous moral choices and exercises critical reflection, they will have a good summary of the differences between individual and ecological intelligence. They will also have part of the answer as to why so few educational reformers are able to propose reforms that address the cultural roots of the ecological crises.

References

Bateson, G. (1972). *Steps to an ecology of mind.* New York: Ballantine Books.

Bateson, G. (1979). *Mind and nature.* New York: Bantam Books.

Bowers, C. (2002). Toward an eco-justice pedagogy. *Environmental Education Research, 8*(1), 21–34.

Bowers, C. (2011). *Perspectives on the ideas of Gregory Bateson, ecological intelligence, and educational reforms*. Eugene, OR: Eco-Justice Press.

Freire, P. (1970). *Pedagogy of the oppressed*. New York: Continuum.

Gadotti, M. (2002). *Pedagogy of the earth and culture of sustainability*. Sao-Paulo, Brazil: Instituto Paulo Freire.

Kahn, R. (2010). *Critical pedagogy, ecoliteracy, & planetary crisis*. New York: Peter Lang.

Lakoff, M., & Johnson, M. (1999). *Philosophy in the flesh: the embodied mind and its challenge to western philosophers*. Chicago, IL: University of Chicago Press.

Ong, W. (1982). *Orality and literacy: the technologizing of the word*. New York: Methuen.

Snyder, G. (1990). *The practice of the wild*. San Francisco, CA: North Point Press.

Reclaiming our moral agency through healing: a call to moral, social, environmental activists

Heesoon Bai
Simon Fraser University, Canada

This paper makes the case that environmental education needs to be taken up as a moral education to the extent that we see the connection between harm and destruction in the environment and harm and destruction within human individuals and their relationship, and proceeds to show this connection by introducing the key notion of human alienation and its psychological factors of wounding, dissociation or split, self and other oppression and exploitation, all of which result in compromised moral agency. To this end, the paper further makes the case that we need to replace the culture of alienation with a culture of healing and reclamation of fundamental humanity manifest as compassion and wisdom, and presents an ideal of moral agency that would emerge when all parts and dimensions of one's being—body–mind–heart–energetics—are aligned, attuned and integrated, having healed from the body–mind split, mind–heart split, body–spirit split and mind–matter split. Concepts and imagery borrowed from Asian philosophies, such as Buddhism and Daoism, are offered as illustrative resources for the project of reclaiming uncompromised moral agency and its manifestation through compassion and wisdom. These concepts include *hungry ghosts, bodhicitta, sunyata* and *wu-wei.*

Environment is *us*

Fundamentally, environmental problems are *us*—the manner of our presence in the world. By saying 'us' I mean to implicate all of us humans, including myself. By virtue of participating in the industrialised and militarised world order that pollutes and destroys the air, water, land and human communities, each and every one of us is complicit in various ways and degrees in creating natural and human environmental problems. To the degree to which we are not awakened to the reality of interdependency and to our unwitting participation in what is happening to the world, and to the degree to which we are not courageous enough to take responsibility for our manner of being in the world, to that degree we are compromised moral agents.

Parker Palmer has gifted us with the famous line, 'We teach who we are' (1998, p. 1), and Cohen gave it an incisive twist: 'We teach who we are, and that's the problem' (2009, p. 27). We can replace 'teach' with many other action words and the essential meaning of the statement is the same. Our actions in the world emanate from *who we are*: the way we think, perceive, sense and feel. The landscape outside reflects our inner landscape, and environmental problems reflect the disorder of the human mind (Schumacher, 1999; Orr, 1994). If the world that resulted from our intense interaction over time is riddled with problems, then the first order of action we need to take is re-searching ourselves and changing who (or how) we are. Yet it seems that is not how most us are educated to think. We look at the problem-ridden world (that we have created), and the first and often only thing we think of is doing something to the environment to fix it without recognising how we created and contributed to the problem by thinking, perceiving and acting in certain ways. The subtext to this *modus operandi* seems to be that we fix and change the world so that we do not have to change ourselves and can go on being and acting the way we have been. I propose that this very way of externalising problems, based on thinking dualistically in terms of the inner–outer separation, is the fundamental problem that we the environmental educators are called to address.

The understanding that fundamentally environmental problems are not the problems *of* the environment (although *in* the environment) but of current humanity is becoming increasingly an accepted position among many contemporary environmental educators and activists. My observation is that this understanding has yet to take root in the minds of the general public. I have a couple of anecdotal accounts to share. In the mid-nineties, I had my graduate class read Orr's book, *Earth in mind* (1994). In the Introduction Orr asserts: 'The disordering of ecological systems and of the great biogeochemical cycles of the earth reflects a prior disorder in the thought, perception, imagination, intellectual priorities, and loyalties inherent in the industrial mind' (p. 3). My students, many of whom were dedicated environmental educators in their schools, thought that Orr was off the mark in locating the environmental problems in humans when, clearly, the environment needed clean-up, repair and conservation. Today, 15 years later, most of the graduate students I teach in the same course are convinced that we need to work on ourselves, and change our consciousness: our mind–body–heart–spirit. They are seeing this work of changing our consciousness as seamlessly integrated with sustainable environmental actions. They are eager to be introduced to ways of thinking and living that will shift their consciousness from the problematic industrial–military–consumeristic mindset to one that is ecological, holistic, compassionate and aligned with the earth. Ecopsychologist Metzner's message that '[w]hat individuals and groups can do … is to change their relationship to Earth and the ecosystem in which they live—and this would contribute to the healing of Earth as a whole' (1999, p. 35) is embraced wholeheartedly by my students. I am heartened by this shift in philosophical and political orientation that I am witnessing in my graduate student population. I am also aware that they struggle to enact this shift in thinking in their daily professional practice in institutions and in their personal lives. I validate their struggle: it is my struggle too.

In another context of interaction, however, I recently came away astonished and disheartened from listening to a panel discussion on a green economy. The expert panel gathered some of the most successful green entrepreneurs local to Vancouver where I live. These were CEOs, directors, presidents and inventors in companies that market and manage products that create and support a green economy. The panel quoted the Globe Foundation Report on British Columbia's Green Economy:

> GDP from [British Columbia's] green sectors could grow from $15.3 billion in 2009 to between $20.1 billion and $27.4 billion in 2020. ... With an average annual green labour force growth rate of 2.6 percent, direct and indirect [full-time equivalent] jobs in BC's green economy would grow 1666,000 in 2008 to 225,000 by 2020. (Globe Foundation, 2010, p. 15)

I was impressed and pleased. At the same time, as I listened to the panel, I was struck by the uniformity of modernist worldview and mindset that prevailed. The modernist worldview and mindset is one that categorically separates self the subject from Nature the object and sees the former's role to be exercising mastery and domination over the latter (Smart, 1993). Amongst the panellists, there was not one mention of changing our mindset, consciousness, paradigm, orientation, worldview, values and ways of being! This was astonishing to me. The closest the panel came to mentioning human subjectivity was a remark by one panellist who declared that he was pessimistic about human nature but optimistic about technology. I guessed that he was entertaining the classic notion of 'human nature' as being fixed (and probably, 'dark', as in Hobbes), and that this person did not think we could do anything about human nature to effect environmental changes. Coming from this viewpoint, he understandably decided to put all his energy and effort into technological innovations to bring about desired environmental changes. He was not alone in this way of thinking: for all the panellists, changing and improving the world was a matter of using greener technology and doing greener resource management.

I bow to the effort and achievement of the panel: citizens in the province and beyond have all benefitted tremendously from their generous and smart actions. However, the panel left me deeply troubled and thoughtful. It is not what they were able to achieve that troubled me. It was what was *not* addressed: greening our consciousness and changing the destructive inner landscape. Joanna Macy (2000) puts it this way: 'Action is not something you do. It's something you are' (p. 253). Greening of our inner landscape was not mentioned because, I surmise, to the panellists it was outside their vision or control. People cannot change what they do not notice or have little control over. Could it be that people are not recognising that their inner landscape has been shaped and conditioned to exclude thinking of greening consciousness? Could it be that for these panellists and many others in our society, the notion of being able to exert the same degree of control over one's inner landscape as over one's physical environment is a foreign notion?

And that this inability to work with the inner landscape—the shape of one's subjectivity—is precisely a major part of environmental problems? I wish to pursue this line of thinking in the present paper.

I draw upon Asian philosophies, especially Buddhism and Daoism, as well as existential psychotherapy to help me see and articulate the environmental problem as a moral, cultural and spiritual problem. Students of Buddhism may name the present rapacious and insatiable humanity that keeps devouring the world resources and each other as 'hungry ghosts'; in psychotherapy we call it alienated subjectivity. I wish to examine in depth this issue of 'human nature' and human presence that has become a singularly destructive force, and that, according to many, cannot be changed. I wish to challenge the underlying assumptions about human nature by uncovering its wounded origin and finding ways to heal it. To me this healing is the primary task today of environmental education as moral education, and moral education as cultural and spiritual education. I shall make the meaning of 'moral', 'cultural' and 'spiritual' more explicit in the pages to come.

Hungry ghosts

One of the life-changing books I read not long after I immigrated to Canada in the 1970s was *The limits to growth* (Meadows, 1972). The author and associated researchers behind this project, backed up by extant research and the best simulation modelling available in those days, indicated that, if the existing trend of human systems (e.g. population increase, industrialisation and concomitant production/consumption growth, pollution, food production and resource depletion) continued, it would overtake the earth's carrying capacity, and by the twenty-first century, the world would face serious survival challenges both for humans and the rest of the planet. Did we heed the warning, then? No. The Wheel of Progress kept turning, and we kept marching on, like sleepwalkers.

The limits of growth faced some severe criticisms and dismissal from both the public and the scientific community when it first came out. The work was attacked and dismissed as '"an empty and misleading work … and smelling of chicanery"' and further ridiculed with a remark: '"an extrapolation of the trends of the 1880s would show today's cities buried under horse manure"' (Passell et al., as quoted in Atkisson, 1999, p. 14). The methodology, database and variables used for modelling the consequences of an exponentially growing world population and finite resources, as well as the motives behind the authors, were all criticised. Henry C. Wallich, Yale economist, accused the work as a publicity stunt, and assured the public that 'technology could solve all the problems [the authors] were concerned about, but only if growth continued apace' (The limits to growth, n.d., para. # 11). Now it appears that its original 'predictions' are being largely validated (Turner, 2008). Today, the same warning about limits to growth in human systems is heard, but this time the warning signals an imminent disaster like an ambulance or fire truck siren. Are we taking immediate action to avoid disaster? No, not really. Many, including Lovelock (2009), believe that it is too late now to turn our civilisation around and avoid disaster. The collapse is imminent. I will not join the technical debate regarding the whether and when of the collapse. My father, a Traditional Oriental Medicine doctor, never refused to see patients as long as they were still alive and breathing, and my father did his best to help the ill and distressed, regardless of the future outcome. Our species' death may be imminent, but we are not dead yet. Speaking as a physician's daughter, I say, it is never too late to extend care and healing to suffering patients.

I have been for a long time trying to make sense of why people (including myself) do not easily change their destructive ways of being, even in the face of impending danger and harm. Addiction is a classic example. An insight for my inquiry into humanity's resistance to change initially came from my Buddhist studies, and now I also have the chance to see how this insight is corroborated by psychotherapy. Buddhism posits the core state of humanity to be unconditioned goodness. (As we shall see later, this understanding is not speculative and theoretical; it is experiential.) This is the primal or *aboriginal* state of humanity, and it is known in Buddhism as *bodhicitta*, enlightened consciousness that is full of compassion and wisdom. *Bodhicitta* exists as a potential capacity for all humans (and according to Buddhism, for all sentient beings). In this sense, it is our birthright. However, potential is not actual. Capacity remains only as potential unless it is given the opportunity to be developed and realised.

Opportunities to fully develop and manifest *bodhicitta* are, however, not easily and amply available in a culture entrenched in anxiety, insecurity and fear associated with individualistic survival stress and competition. Soon after birth (or even prenatal), many babies receive distorted or ruptured forms of attachment (Bowlby, 1988; Neufeld & Maté, 2005; Winnicott, 1964; Winnicott, Winnicott, Shepherd, & Davis, 1984), which compromises the manifestation of *bodhicitta*. Psychological and psychotherapeutic literature is replete with research details about infant bonding rupture and insecure attachment in young children, as well as parenting, socialisation, and education practices that build, even if unwittingly, not open-heartedness, compassion and collaboration but jealousy, greed, enmity and self- and other destructive behaviour (Miller, 1987/2005, 2009; Schellenbaum, 1988/1990; Siegel & Solomon, 2003).

To briefly explain psychodynamically this *bodhicitta* manifestation: human individuals, especially during their early bonding period of growth, thrive when they have unconditionally loving and wisely caring others who are fully present to them, and who attentively listen for their needs, validate their experience, and interact with them in ways that are conducive to their developing into secure and confident persons, ready to encounter and embrace the world with warmth, courage, curiosity and confidence. That is the way of the open-mind and open-heart. However, to the extent this process is disrupted and thwarted, and we become psychologically wounded and scarred beings, to that extent our aboriginal nature as *bodhicitta* does not manifest itself fully or readily. The result of such thwarting is compromised or even arrested growth as ontologically secure, confident and compassionate human beings. In fact, we insidiously develop distorted and defensive personality structures and patterns that are seamlessly interlocked with emotional and physical patterns that we ignorantly think of as our authentic identity (Cohen, 2009).

The entire defence configuration actually serves the purpose of protecting what Schneider (2004) describes as the '*fluid center*'. He explains:

> The fluid center is any sphere of human consciousness which has as its concern the widest possible relationship to existence; or to put it another way, it is structured inclusiveness—the richest possible range of experience within the most suitable parameters of support. (p. 10)

Generosity, caring, warm-heartedness, receptivity and empathy and compassion do not flow easily and amply out of human beings when they are unconsciously constructed to protect their fluid centre. This seems to be more or less the case for everyone. As the Buddhist practitioner and psychotherapist David Brazier (1997/2001) observes: 'We all carry hurt within us. It is not possible to have gone through life without getting buffeted' (p. 44).

Fragile and vulnerable infants and children who have no capacity to defend themselves against repeated patterns of intrusion, insult and neglect—albeit by mostly very well-meaning parents and authority figures—will manifest the psychological defence structures in order to survive and to get at least some morsels of the love that they need for survival (Schellenbaum, 1990). In the process, their moral agency is more or less compromised. How could they manifest what they do not have? These deprived and hurt beings, in turn, are in search of what they did not receive, are missing and not getting: love, compassion, caring, confidence and integrity as human beings, and an inward measure of peace and equanimity.

In Buddhist literature, there is the figure of a hungry ghost, a human figure with impossibly thin, long neck and a needle-like small aperture as mouth and bloated belly. This is how Epstein (1995), contemporary psychiatrist and Buddhist teacher, depicts hungry ghosts:

> Phantom-like creatures with withered limbs, grossly bloated bellies, and long thin necks, the Hungry Ghosts in many ways represent a fusion of rage and desire. Tormented by unfulfilled cravings and insatiably demanding of impossible satisfactions, the Hungry Ghosts are searching for gratification for old unfulfilled needs whose time has passed. They are beings who have uncovered a terrible emptiness within themselves, who cannot see the impossibility of correcting something that has already happened. (p. 28)

Hungry ghosts devour everything in sight, and want more and more, but nothing nourishes them, or nothing they eat has the right nourishment, and they are left hungrier than ever. Please look around; and look deeply within. Are we—most of us—not hungry ghosts in this desire-saturated culture of production and consumption (Kaza, 2005)? Has our culture not normalised this hungry-ghost state of being?

In addition to the Buddhist imagery of the hungry ghost, I also find the existentialist psychotherapeutic language of *alienated subjectivity* to be very pertinent and useful in describing and illuminating the above-mentioned process of privation, wounding and compromised human maturity. I turn to Laing (1967), foremost existential psychotherapist of the twentieth century and outspoken communicator, for his articulation of alienation:

> What we call 'normal' is a product of repression, denial, splitting, projection, introjection and other forms of destructive action on experience ... It is radically estranged from the structure of being ... The condition of alienation, of being asleep, of being unconscious, of being out of one's mind, is the condition of the normal man. (pp. 23–24)

I extrapolate three points from the above: (1) that alienation comes about through negating and invalidating an individual's experience, hence subjectivity, that results in his/her estrangement from the 'structure of being'; (2) that a person suffering from alienation has compromised moral agency and therefore limited capacity for responsibility; and (3) that alienation is normalised in our culture and society. In the following pages, I shall attempt to further explore and elaborate these three points.

I turn to Laing (1967) again for his insight into the aetiology of alienated human subjectivity that has been normalised in our modern civilisation, and the destructive consequences of alienation. Laing states: 'Much of human behaviour can be seen as unilateral or bilateral attempts to eliminate experience. A person may treat another as though he was not a person, and he may act himself as though he was not a person' (1967, p. 22). How do we eliminate experience? By not respectfully and sensitively receiving and acknowledging another's expression of experience, thereby their presence. This can take many forms, including: denying, ignoring, dismissing, invalidating, trivialising and/or ridiculing it. Of course, this type of reactivity is not just reserved for others. Having been treated in invalidating ways ourselves, we may well have incorporated these ways unconsciously into our sense of identity, and this has the consequence of subjecting ourselves and our own thoughts and feelings to the same forms of invalidation. Because we are fundamentally intersubjective beings, how we are received, understood and treated by others matters crucially to our sense of self and our reality. When a growing and evolving person is not heard, seen, or met with by another in a fully attentive and caring way, that person's subjectivity, which I have been referring to as 'inner landscape', is likely to become eroded and distorted, her sense of self-worth becomes diminished and even wounded, and her confidence and ontological security is compromised. 'There seems to be no agent more effective than another person in bringing a world for oneself alive, or, by a glance, a gesture, or a remark, shrivelling up the reality in which one is lodged' (Goffman, as cited in Laing, 1967, p. 28). Repeated patterns of abuse to and/or neglect of subjectivity will lead to wounding and crippling of the young person's psyche (Miller, 1987/2005; Schellenbaum, 1988/1990).

As illustrations I present two vignettes here. Suppose a little boy cries, feeling upset and sad at losing his pet goldfish, and his mother or father says, 'Boys don't cry! Don't be a sissy. Now, just go and flush that ugly sight down the toilet!'. The boy learns then that in order for him not to be an embarrassment to his parents, and to continue to win their approval, esteem, love and acceptance, he would need to suppress his emotions, especially tender sorrowful emotions, and pretend that he is emotionally tough. This 'tough' lesson may continue in his school and in his neighbourhood. Being a 'good boy' (he 'instinctively' knows that he needs to be a 'good boy' to win his parents' and teachers' support and care), he learns the lesson well, he may even demonstrate his competence in toughness by being disrespectful and insensitive, and even cruel, to other vulnerable people, other sentient beings and objects. By this process, gradually he may become disconnected from those emotions that express tenderness towards the marginalised and vulnerable, and compassion for the hurt and suffering.

Similarly, suppose a mother turns to her son and says, 'Don't hang out with children who get low grades. They are losers. Only smart people succeed these days. The world is getting really competitive.' This son, out of fear of disapproval and losing parental love and out of survival anxiety, may learn to separate mind/intellect from heart/emotion, and prioritise the former over the latter, thus devaluing the latter. This person may become a successful surgeon, engineer, lawyer, business leader, or accountant, but his capacity for compassion is limited, and he may not think much about suffering others, including non-human others who, in their understanding, lack intelligence or rationality.

The above vignettes are not intended to somehow prove that everyone who has been unkindly and insensitively treated as children will become insensitive, and lack empathy and compassion. Rather, I offer these vignettes as a lens through which to view the present world and see the underlying psychological reality—the inner landscape of alienated human beings. At the present moment, the planet abounds with human beings who have learned to see non-human sentient beings merely or mostly as objects, as resources that satisfy human desires but not as beings that live for themselves, that are subjects unto themselves, and worthy of our fundamental respect (Bai, 2001; Bai & Scutt, 2009). Likewise, the planet also abounds with human beings who see other humans as failures, distortions and perversions, and therefore not worthy and deserving of one's respect and care. Many also have learned to see their own self in the same dark light. Or, even as exploitable resources that exist to provide goods and services to privileged others. All these are instances of alienated subjectivity. As we saw, alienated subjectivity is a product of ruptured intersubjectivity, meaning that *communion* did not take place between experiencing subjects.

Arguably, alienation is normalised in the world today. Yet, sooner or later, many of us come to our senses enough to feel the pain and horror of alienation deep within ourselves. For example:

> When our personal worlds are rediscovered and allowed to reconstitute themselves, we first discover a shambles. Bodies half-dead; genitals dissociated from heart; heart severed from head; heads dissociated from genitals. Without inner unity, with just enough sense of continuity to clutch at identity—the current idolatry. Torn, body, mind and spirit, by inner contradictions, pulled in different directions, Man cut off from his own

> mind, cut off equally from his own body—a half-crazed creature in a mad world. (Laing, 1967, pp. 46–47)

These are outspoken and dramatic words, and many of us may not readily resonate with them. Bodies half-dead? We would become defensive and cry out, 'Surely, this is not me!'. Let us meditate upon what Laing is getting at: there is an impeccable psycho-logic to this. In the way of living beings, what is not properly and adequately attended to, and cared for, dies. Splitting the whole human being into mind and body, thereby violating the integrity of the person, and then disrespecting the body (human bodies, animal or plant bodies) by teaching us that body is lesser than mind, is not as important, is made of 'meat', is just a piece of machinery, or even 'sinful' and so on, would result in neglected, misunderstood, abused, 'half-dead' bodies.

Genitals dissociated from heart? Another splitting similar to the mind–body split is the body–emotion split. When this split happens, for example, we may have sex without love, which may result in much suffering. Another framing well known to us in the context of schooling is the emotion–intellect split. Despite the growing recognition of the importance of emotion to learning today, education is still primarily focused on the development of intellect (Goleman, 1995). Emotions, especially dark or negative ones (e.g. anger, hostility, loneliness, anxiety, sadness), are usually seen as irrelevance and distraction, if not hindrance, to the development of intellect, and therefore are kept out of school as much as possible. To this end, we tend not to encourage personal openness to and expression of emotions, and do not include working with personal emotions as an important part of school learning. In general we learn to ignore and suppress our emotions in schools, and the same learning tends to be reinforced at home and at work. The general outcome is that we grow up emotionally suppressed, if not distorted and stunted. This affects our ability to be fully and skilfully relational with and responsible (the ability to respond appropriately) towards the world, and to feel and live the *interbeing* (Hahn, 1998/2009) with the world. Our predominant mode of interaction with the world today is instrumentalism: the domination of calculative thinking that leads to abuse and exploitation of the world, which is the opposite of being responsible (Bai, 2001, 2004).

Whatever we learn to devalue and suppress in ourselves, we do the same, unconsciously, to human and non-human others. Unless we come to an explicit realisation that we are the way we are, in our thought patterns, feelings, habits and actions, due to prior conditioning and programming in alienation that we have received from our culture and family of origin, we tend to live and act out of alienated consciousness, and in turn spread, unconsciously, more alienation (Laing, 1980; Loy, 2008; Metzner, 1999). It is, I suggest, this unconsciousness (in degrees) that prevents us from fully taking responsibility as moral agents, and deliberately and decisively enacting changes to heal the damaged inner and outer landscapes.

The enlightenment that Buddhism talks about is waking up from our own unconsciousness about alienation. Unless we can wake up from our conditioning and programming, we will be likely to perform, in turn, the same process upon another human being, especially upon our own vulnerable young children and others under their leadership. This, I believe, is the origin of continuing oppression and exploitation of human and non-human others.

To summarise the main thrust of my arguments so far: environmental educators are moral educators, and moral educators are psychological educators, and all three are cultural educators. What I am trying to convey with this seemingly convoluted statement here is this:

(a) Environmental education needs to be taken up as a moral education to the extent that we see the connection between harm and destruction in the environment and harm and destruction within human individuals and in their relationship.
(b) Environmental education as moral education will need to start with addressing people's alienation (wounding, dissociation, self- and other oppression, instrumentalism and exploitation).
(c) Addressing alienation is a healing (etymologically, *therapy* means healing) work that needs to be taken up not only by the expert professionals (psychotherapists and counsellors) but also by educators in all walks of life, from parents to teachers, from self to leaders.
(d) Healing from alienation is a cultural work in that we need to engage in it collectively through relationship building and community development (Cohen, 2009). We need to replace the culture of alienation (that results in insatiably rapacious hungry ghosts roaming the planet) by a culture of healing and reclamation of fundamental human integrity and dignity, wisdom and compassion.

Now, supposing that we are convinced of the above points, a pressing question for us educators is: how do we put the above proposals into practice? I suggest that the question of 'how' involves finding helpful resources with which we transform our selves and daily lives. In other words, we need to re-*source* ourselves. The good news is that such resources with which we can re-source ourselves abound in many wisdom traditions of the world. In the rest of the paper, I wish to share some resources that derive from some concepts and attendant practices of the Buddhist and the Daoist traditions.

Resources from Eastern sources

Bodhicitta

Robert Thurman, influential scholar of Buddhism and writer, has captured the essence of the Buddha's teaching: an educational programme dedicated to transforming human consciousness at its roots (Thurman, 1998). The central part of this transformation is helping people to get in touch with *bodhicitta*—the core humanity of passion and compassion—and fully manifesting it in everyday life

(Brazier, 1997/2001). Earlier I stated that *bodhicitta* is a human birthright, meaning that it is a fundamental human capacity. The whole meditation tradition in all branches of Buddhism is focused on finding ways to get in touch with the seed of *bodhicitta*, watering it and growing it. The Vietnamese Buddhist monk in exile in France and Nobel Peace Prize nominee, Thich Nhat Hahn, is famous for using the metaphorical language of 'watering the seed' (1991). For many of us who have been heavily conditioned to a modern life of alienation and its ego-driven successes, the seed may be still dormant or has not grown beyond the seedling stage. We search our consciousness, and may find nothing like luxuriantly growing *bodhicitta*. Often all we find may be an onrush of anxiety, fear, frustration, jealousy, feelings of inadequacy, discontent, ill will, anger and hatred, and the attendant turmoil, confusion, despair, self- and other loathing, empty feelings, or wishes that things are otherwise, and resulting tension and despair, helplessness and dispiritedness. Where is this boundlessly warm and radiant, spirited and courageous, at the same time, clear-sighted and calm, loving and compassionate consciousness?

Buddhist teachers talk about catching fleeting glimpses of *bodhicitta* consciousness naturally occurring in our daily lives, and extending or stabilising these glimpses into more enduring experiences. My personal list of such moments probably would elicit resonances from the reader: looking into a wide-eyed baby face, gazing into loved ones' eyes, beholding first spring flowers bursting through the still half-frozen ground, looking up into the vast cloudless sky, and so on. The next step to noticing a *bodhicitta* moment is intentionally extending the experience by lingering and dwelling in it rather than the usual cognitive habit of quickly moving on. Extension is a powerful learning principle well known in ancient China (Kupperman, 1999) as is today in cognitive science (Varela, 1999). Not surprisingly, this principle of noticing what is already there (in our case, the *bodhicitta* moments) and extending it constitutes the most practical instruction on meditation (Sogyal Rinpoche, 2002). Meditation teachers with whom I have worked in the past would give a sitting meditation instruction of finding a moment of gap between two discrete thought events, and extending the gap by staying in it longer and longer. It is not easy to communicate about a subjective experience, and I am struggling to find a way to do so here. Perhaps I can suggest to the reader to think of, or better yet to try, extending the lengths of their in-breaths and out-breaths. I suggest that this experience of extending each breath is similar to the experience of extending the gap between cognitive-events in meditation.

The moment of gap between thoughts (cognitive content) is experienced as the source of *bodhicitta*—the ontological space of unconditioned and spacious stillness that is full of warm and radiant energy. This ontological space is understood in Buddhism as the matrix of human consciousness, and therefore the source of human wisdom and compassion. With regular practice of touching *bodhicitta* and extending these moments, we may be able to establish ourselves in a steady state of *bodhicitta* consciousness. We may expect three things to happen over time: (1) *bodhicitta* becomes the permanent background consciousness that can be brought to the foreground at will; (2) we can take refuge in *bodhicitta* anytime and take a break from the usual conditioned consciousness that compels us to think, feel and react in particular ways that are not life-nourishing and dignity and integrity promoting; (3) aided by *bodhicitta*, we may change our conditioned patterns of thought and feeling that are manifestations of our alienated subjectivity, and feel more integrated, fluid, connected, authentic and alive. As a practitioner of *bodhicitta*, I find these three points to be powerfully helpful for healing my own alienated subjectivity and encouraging me to gain confidence in the primordial level of my being and awareness (Ray, 2008). I propose that the cultivation of *bodhicitta* is the way to work with—nourish and nurture—the *hungry ghosts* within each of us.

Sunyata

There is the tendency in the modern Western traditions of moral education to mainly focus on the *content* of moral teaching in the sense that we want our learners to acquire specific discursive moral teachings and competencies, be they moral concepts, rules, imperatives, reasoning, judgement, criteria, evaluation, stories, virtues or character. In contrast, the approach I have taken in this paper, based on my studies of Buddhism and Daoism, is focused primarily on the 'ontological space' around the discursive content of consciousness: that is, the 'container' itself. This space or container is mostly invisible to us in our daily lives precisely because we are most often singularly focused on the discursive content, of which there are endless torrents. When we are so immersed in the details of the content, we lose sight of the empty (i.e. non-discursive) space that holds the content. The experience here may be likened to walking into a room so completely filled up with things that one does not see the space: all one sees are the things. In the Buddhist understanding and practice, the discursively empty 'space' is the field of *bodhicitta*. Hence, the notion of emptiness, *sunyata* (means zero, nothing), plays a crucial role in Buddhist theory and practice, and Far Eastern cultures in general (Suzuki, 1959).

I now wish to probe the importance of *sunyata* for our moral–environmental–cultural education, suggesting that emptiness *as experience* yields some very important insights for us:

(1) Being highly languaged beings, we tend to take our words and the ideas behind them too literally. When we do that, we forget that words and ideas are human inventions and devices, and that, as such, we need to take responsibility for our use of them rather than seeing them as 'Truth' and 'Reality'. The result of taking our words and concepts as 'Truth' and 'Reality' is, I suggest, fundamentalism, of which we have a whole variety: religious fundamentalism, ethnic fundamentalism, economic fundamentalism, and so on. I would like to add 'moral fundamentalism' to the list. Anytime we find people ready to go to war and kill (invalidate, marginalise, silence, dehumanise, punish) others who are holding other or opposite

moral views, we should know that we are dealing with a case of fundamentalism. Moral fundamentalists are those who are so focused on what is right (moral, good) and wrong (immoral, evil) that they neglect to wonder whether there are different ways of understanding what is right and wrong, good or bad. And more seriously, they fail to exercise empathy and compassion in understanding different others who may be in difficulties, and providing support to them. Predictably, when faced with different others and their ways, moral fundamentalists react by condemning, marginalising and punishing those who transgress. Moral fundamentalists' need to be 'right' and 'good' overwhelms them such that they have little room for understanding others and interacting with them in ways that will foster peace and harmony.

But if we could see that words do not mirror reality (Rorty, 1979/2009), and that their relationship to reality is *subjunctive*, not literal, then, I suspect, we would not be so militantly rigid and insistent about the right and the wrong of our views. Reality is far bigger than what anyone can name with his or her words. Being mindful of this, we may cultivate a subjunctive relationship with words. We may speak *as if* our words name some truths; we may listen to others *as if* their words are right, and so on. We need not be committed to our or their words once and for all, objectively and forever. I admit that this subjunctive attitude is difficult to cultivate. This is where experience of *sunyata* would be helpful as it would have us realise that reality is *fundamentally ineffable*, and that all our ideas, concepts and words are fingers pointing to the moon, not the moon itself, to use the well-known zennist metaphor. Our job, especially as educators, is to find helpful fingers, but not to mistake fingers for the moon, and fight, and train others to fight, over the fingers.

(2) *Sunyata* also points to the need to regularly empty ourselves of fixed notions, power struggles, judgemental attitudes, and other ego preoccupations that mark the phenomenal plane of human existence, in order to support and experience the ample arising of *bodhicitta*. Of course, again, 'emptying' is not to be taken in absolute or even literal terms. 'Emptiness' and 'fullness' are polar terms, as in *yin* and *yang*. Human consciousness is always in dynamic flux of emptiness/fullness (Cheng, 1994). It is when we are held captive by thoughts, ideas, information, knowledge, plans, desire, goals, objectives, agendas, and so on, that we have difficulty experiencing *sunyata*—the spaciousness of the mindheart. My experience is that without being able to experience some measure of *sunyata*, it is difficult to experience the spontaneous arising of *bodhicitta*. Hence, I suggest that moral (social, environmental) education based on getting in touch with *bodhicitta* would need to be careful about doing the usual, which is discursively filling people up with moral principles, rules, imperatives and virtues, and compelling them to act. It is not that these morals are bad or useless: they are most often helpful and useful.

But if we are mainly focused on these, then we may neglect to connect with the source of compassion and wisdom: *bodhicitta*.

Wu-wei moral agency

As a last resource, I wish to introduce another related concept from the Eastern tradition: the Daoist concept of *wu-wei*. *Wu-wei* means 'no (wu) effort/work (wei).' Like *sunyata*, *wu-wei* is a concept of negation. However, *wu-wei* does not mean that one does nothing. Rather, it negates stressful and strained effort-making or work: doing too much, producing too much, consuming too much, and in general pushing and straining oneself and others until we are beyond limits and out of balance. Arguably, today the world has gone to the opposite direction of *wu-wei*, and the result is a civilisation that is egregiously straining the carrying capacity of the biosphere and the caring capacity of humans. In my view, much harm and damage in the world come from such rapacious energy and action. Given this, *wu-wei* may offer a paradigm of moral agency that does not fuel the relentlessly grinding engine of our industrial–consumer–military civilisation.

Wu-wei is a complex and demanding concept. *Wu-wei* agency requires knowing when is 'just enough' and optimal in one's action. This in turn requires us to study and know the environment and the objects/beings within it, including, of course, one's self, very closely and carefully to the point that we have an intimate understanding of not only the interconnected parts of what we study but also the whole dynamic system and its residing genius. There is a famous story of the cook Ting who was able to cut up a whole ox without dulling his knife blade (Chuang Tze, 1964). When asked what his secret was, his reply was that he did not need to look at the ox anymore, but just followed the 'way' of the animal in front of him, implying that he knew the animal so intimately that all he had to do was just thrust his knife blade into the hollow space between joints, never hitting bones or ligaments. Optimal effort is what *wu-wei* agency is about, and thus is a paradigm of action that would be a corrective to the kind of more-is-better, bigger-is-better, faster-is-better, aggressive and rapacious agency that dominates the world today. Insofar as the latter kind of agency is stressing us out and burning up the world, *wu-wei* is an antidote and re-balancing moral agency that we are well to adopt and adapt in some form in support of more ecological and sustainable living.

As indicated, no one can practice *wu-wei* without cultivating an acute power of observation and listening, sensitivity, intimate knowing of self, other and world, and a highly attuned feeling and knowing in-the-moment, each and every moment. All of this requires one to be supremely relational with the world. Here, too, the support for the *wu-wei* agency is the same as *bodhicitta*: *sunyata*. *Sunyata* allows us to be unfettered enough that we can really pay attention to what is before and around us and notice, rather than being continually compelled by the pre-given mental constructs and habits that make up our ordinary identity. This process of learning to let go of agenda and of letting be, so as to be able to pay attention to whatever arises in the moment is what *zazen* (literally, seated meditation) practice of 'just sitting' meditation is about. Through *just sitting* and other related practices that liberate us from the restless and aggressive energy that knows no limit, contentment and fulfilment, we learn to dwell in the moment, making peace with the world and our selves, and living in harmony.

As an educator, I have taken Parker Palmer's message of 'We teach who we are' (1998, p. 1) to heart; I have also taken Cohen's addition of 'We teach who we are, and that's the problem' (2009, p. 27) to heart. For me, taking these messages to heart means daily engaging in my own self-healing and self-cultivation (Bai, 2012) so that when I go into my class I can speak from a place of mind–body–heart–spirit integrity-in-the-making, and offer my own self and life as a resource, including my own mistakes, limitations and struggles for my students' learning.

Acknowledgements

I express my thanks to the anonymous reviewers for their helpful feedback and reviews, and my deep gratitude and appreciation for the Special Issue Editor, Dr Michael Bonnett, for his attentive support throughout this article's long gestation and creation. And also a very special note of appreciation for Dr Monica Taylor, the retiring *JME* Editor, for her warm support and leadership.

References

Atkisson, A. (1999). When worlds collapse. Available online at: http://www.isisacademy.com/wp-content/uploads/Believing_Cassandra_Chapter1_and_Prelims.pdf (accessed 17 April 2012).

Bai, H. (2001). Challenge for education: Learning to value the world intrinsically. *Encounter, 14* (1), 4–16.

Bai, H. (2004). The three I's for ethics as an everyday activity: Integration, intrinsic valuing, and intersubjectivity. *Canadian Journal of Environmental Education, 9*, 51–64.

Bai, H. (2012). Education for enlightenment. In A. Cohen, M. Porath, A. Clarke, H. Bai, C. Leggo, & K. Meyer (co-authors). *Speaking of teaching: Inclinations, inspirations, and innerworkings*. Rotterdam, The Netherlands: Sense Publishers.

Bai, H., & Scutt, G. (2009). Touching the earth with the heart of enlightened mind: A Buddhist contribution to ecology as educational practice. *Canadian Journal of Environmental Education, 14*, 92–106.

Bowlby, J. (1988). *A secure base: Parent–child attachment and healthy human development*. London: Basic Books.

Brazier, D. (1997/2001). *The feeling Buddha: A Buddhist psychology of character, adversity and passion*. New York: Palgrave.

Cheng, F. (1994). *Empty and full: The language of Chinese painting*, trans. M.H. Kohn. Boston, MA: Shambhala Publications.

Chuang Tze (1964). *The basic writings*, trans. B. Watson. New York: Columbia University Press.

Cohen, A. (2009). *Gateway to the Dao-field: Essays for the awakening educator*. New York: Cambria Press.

Epstein, M. (1995). *Thoughts without a thinker: Psychotherapy from a Buddhist perspective*. New York: Basic Books.

Globe Foundation (2010). Building a strong carbon future. Available online at: http://bcgreeneconomy.globeadvisors.ca/media/227/bcge_report_feb_2010.pdf (accessed 17 April 2012).

Goleman, D. (1995). *Emotional intelligence*. New York: Bantam Books.

Hahn, T. (1991). *Peace is every step: The path of mindfulness*. New York: Bantam Books.

Hahn, T. (1998/2009). *The heart of understanding: Commentaries on the Prajnaparamita Heart Sutra*. Berkeley, CA: Parallax Press.

Kaza, S. (2005). *Hooked: Buddhist writings on greed, desire, and the urge to consume*. Boston, MA: Shambhala Publications.

Kupperman, J. (1999). *Learning from Asian philosophy*. London: Oxford University Press.

Laing, R.D. (1967). *The politics of experience and the bird of paradise*. Harmondsworth, Middlesex: Penguin Books.

Laing, R.D. (1980). What is the matter with mind? In S. Kumar (Ed.), *The Schumacher lectures* (pp. 1–27). London: Sphere Books.

Lovelock, J. (2009). *The vanishing face of Gaia: A final warning*. Toronto, ON: Penguin.

Loy, D.R. (2008). *Money, sex, warm, karma: Notes for a Buddhist revolution*. Boston, MA: Wisdom Publications.

Macy, J. (2000). Encouraging words for activists. In S. Kaza & K. Kraft (Eds.), *Dharma rain: Sources of Buddhist environmentalism* (pp. 252–256). Boston, MA: Shambhala Publications.

Meadows, D. (1972). *The limits to growth*. New York: The New American Library.

Metzner, R. (1999). *Green psychology: Transforming our relationship to the Earth*. Rochester, VT: Park Street Press.

Miller, A. (1987/2005). *The drama of being a child: The search for the true self*. London: Virago.

Miller, A. (2009). *Free from lies: discovering your true needs*, trans. A. Jenkins. New York: W.W. Norton & Company.

Neufeld, G., & Maté, G. (2005). *Hold on to your kids: Why parents need to matter more than peers*. New York: Ballantine Books.

Orr, D. (1994). *Earth in mind: On education, environment, and the human prospect*. Washington, DC: Island Press.

Palmer, J.P. (1998). *Courage to teach: Exploring the inner landscape of a teacher's life*. San Francisco, CA: Jossey-Bass.

Ray, R. (2008). *Touching enlightenment: Finding realization in the body*. Boulder, CO: Sounds True.

Rorty, R. (1979/2009). *Philosophy and the mirror of nature* (thirthieth-anniversary edition). Princeton, NJ: Princeton University Press.

Schellenbaum, P. (1988/1990). *The wound of the unloved: Releasing the life energy*, trans. T. Nevill. Sturminster Newton, UK: Element Books.

Schneider, K. (2004). *Rediscovery of awe: Splendor, mystery, and the fluid center of life*. St. Paul, MN: Paragon House.

Schumacher, E.F. (1999). *Small is beautiful: Economics as if people mattered*. Point Roberts, WA: Hartley & Marks Publishers.

Siegel, D.J., & Solomon, M. (2003). *Healing trauma: Attachment, mind, body, and brain*. New York: W.W. Norton & Company.

Smart, B. (1993). *Postmodernity*. London: Routledge.

Sogyal, Rinpoche. (2002). *The Tibetan book of living and dying*. New York: HarperCollins.

Suzuki, D.T. (1959). *Zen and Japanese culture*. New York: Bollingen Foundation.

The limits to growth. (n.d.). Available online at: http://en.wikipedia.org/wiki/The_Limits_to_Growth (accessed 23 May 2011).

Thurman, R. (1998). *Inner revolution: Life, liberty, and the pursuit of real happiness*. New York: Riverhead Books.

Turner, G. (2008). A comparison of The Limits to Growth with Thirty Years of Reality. Available online at: http://www.csiro.au/files/files/plje.pdf (accessed 17 April 2012).

Varela, F.J. (1999). *Ethical know-how: Action, wisdom, and cognition*. Stanford, CA: Stanford University Press.

Winnicott, D.W. (1964). *The child, the family, and the outside world.* Cambridge, MA: Perseus.

Winnicott, D.W., Winnicott, C., Shepherd, R., & Davis, M. (1984). *Deprivation and delinquency.* London & New York: Tavistock.

Ubuntu, *ukama*, environment and moral education

Lesley Le Grange
University of Stellenbosch, South Africa

This article outlines a moral education guided by African traditional values such as *ubuntu* and *ukama*. It argues that *ubuntu* is not by definition speciesist, as some have claimed, but that it has strong ecocentric leanings, that is, if *ubuntu* is understood as a concrete expression of *ukama*. In fact, *ubuntu* deconstructs the anthropocentric–ecocentric distinction which has characterised and continues to characterise debates in environmental theory/philosophy. To become more fully human does not mean caring only for the self and other human beings but also for the entire biophysical world. Some implications that this discussion has for moral education are explored, as well as some opportunities that post-apartheid curriculum frameworks offer for implementing a moral education guided by *ubuntu*.

Introduction

Environmental problems have reached unprecedented levels to the extent that many (for example, Barry & Eckersley, 2005; Bowers & Apffel-Marglin, 2005; Guattari, 2001) refer to the current state of the global environment as one of crisis. A crisis might be an indication of impending disaster or could indicate a civilisational threshold whereby outmoded thinking and values are replaced by new ones (or where old values are rejuvenated). Whatever the environmental crises might indicate, this brings a perennial existential question to the fore: 'How we should live?' Or, put differently, 'What are our moral obligations?' This article aims to address the latter question by tracing how moral obligation is defined from disparate environmentalist (or non-environmentalist) positions. It further wishes to explore what insights the traditional African value, *ubuntu*, might bring to our understanding of moral obligation *vis-à-vis* non-human nature. Moreover, implications for a moral education guided by *ubuntu* will be explored.

Since the 1960s in particular there has been growing awareness of the impact of human activity on the environment, as evidenced in published works such as those of: Rachel Carson (1962), who was concerned with environmental problems associated with the use of pesticides; Ehrlich and Ehrlich (1970), who were concerned with human population problems; and Meadows, Meadows, Randers, and Behrens (1974), who were concerned with issues related to resources. With hindsight we have become aware of how the transition from the feudal to an industrial economy has resulted in environmental deterioration. The transition involved a shift from the use of renewable energy (human and animal energy) to non-renewable energy (fossil fuels) and the concomitant problem that the combustion of fossils fuels gives rise to air pollution. The German sociologist Ulrich Beck (1992) has argued that risks (including environmental risks) prevalent in the developed world have been produced by science in conjunction with technology. Others have argued that the causes of environmental destruction are linked to values associated with the modern period (modernity), that is, an unquestioning belief in empiricist science and a particular rationality that science (truth) will lead to human progress (Janse van Rensburg, 1994; Schreuder, 1995). We might contest some or all of these claims/positions; however, there is consensus that at least some of the environmental destruction witnessed today is human-induced—that human thinking, beliefs and actions have contributed to environmental destruction. In other words, central to understanding environmental destruction is the nature of relationships/interactions between human beings and non-human nature. This brings us to a debate that has received much attention in the field of environmental ethics over the past few decades; the extent to which non-human nature is a criterion of value—whether non-human nature merely has instrumental value or whether it has intrinsic value.

The extent to which non-human nature is a criterion of value has been the subject of much discussion in environmental philosophy over the years and different positions have been identified. The more familiar categories of anthropocentrism, sentientism, bio-centrism and ecocentrism/holism will be referred to here. There are two broad anthropocentric positions that have been identified: strong anthropocentrism and weak anthropocentrism. Anthropocentrism is the belief that nature only has value insofar it is a means to human ends—that nature has instrumental value. Stronger anthropocentrism holds that nature is to be used to satisfy human needs and interests without necessarily preserving components of the natural world. Weaker anthropocentrism holds that nature is there to serve human interests but parts of nature should be preserved for future human generations, for example. On the opposite side of the spectrum, ecocentrism holds that all of nature has intrinsic value, that nature has value independent of its benefits to human beings. This position is captured very well by the deep ecologist Arne Naess (1984, p. 266) who wrote: 'The well-being of non-human life on Earth has value in itself. This value is independent of any instrumental usefulness for limited human purposes.' There are other positions in between anthropocentrism and ecocentrism. For example, sentientism holds that moral value should be extended to all sentient beings, not just humans. Bio-centrism, although a similar concept to ecocentrism, recognises the moral value of the Earth's organisms, whereas ecocentrism recognises the moral value of the Earth's interactive living and non-living systems.

It is against this background that I will discuss the notion of *ubuntu* and whether it extends moral obligation beyond humans to include the entire biophysical world.

Ubuntu: a linguistic–philosophical concept

Ubuntu/Botho[1] is a concept that is derived from proverbial expressions (aphorisms) found in several languages in Africa south of the Sahara. However, it is not only a linguistic concept but has a normative connotation embodying how we ought to relate to the other—what our moral obligation is towards the other. *Ubuntu* comprises one of the core elements of a human being. In some traditions the African word for human being is *umuntu*, who is constituted by the following: *umzimba* (body, form, flesh); *umoya* (breath, air, life); *umphefumela* (shadow, spirit, soul); *amandla* (vitality, strength, energy); *inhliziyo* (heart, centre of emotions); *umqondo* (head, brain, intellect), *ulwimi* (language, speaking) and *ubuntu* (humanness) (Le Roux, 2000, p. 43). The humanness referred to here finds expression in a communal context rather than the individualism prevalent in many Western societies (Venter, 2004, p. 151). Battle (1996, p. 99) explains the concept *ubuntu* as originating from the Xhosa[2] expression: *Umuntu ngumuntu ngabanye Bantu*, 'Not an easily translatable Xhosa concept, generally, this proverbial expression means that each individual's humanity is ideally expressed in relationship with others and, in turn, individuality is truly expressed'.

Metz and Gaie (2010) argue that there are two ways in which sub-Saharan African morality (as embodied in *ubuntu*) is distinct from Western approaches to morality. Firstly they argue that sub-Saharan morality is essentially relational in the sense that the only way to develop one's humanness is to relate to others in a positive way. In other words, one becomes a person solely through other persons—'one cannot realise one's true self in opposition to others or even in isolation from them' (p. 275). They point out that *ubuntu* means that our deepest moral obligation is to become more fully human and to achieve this requires one to enter more deeply into community with others. One therefore cannot become more fully human or realise one's true self by exploiting, deceiving or acting in unjust ways towards others. Notice how the socious and the self are inextricably bound up within the notion of *ubuntu*. Metz and Gaie (p. 275) argue that the second way in which African morality differs from an Aristotelian or other Western moral philosophy is that it defines positive relationship with others in strictly communal terms. They write:

> One is not to positively relate to others fundamentally by giving them what they deserve, respecting individual human rights grounded on consent, participating in a political sphere or maximising the general welfare, common themes in Western moral philosophy. Instead, the proper way to relate to others, for one large part of sub-Saharan thinking, is to seek out community or to live in harmony with them.

Following from this, moral obligation concerns: doing things for the good of others; to think of oneself as bound up with others; and to value family (in a broad sense of the term) for its own sake and not for its efficacy.

When Metz and Gaie (2010) make reference to the other then they are evidently referring to the *human* other—that relatedness means connectedness with other human beings. In other words, *ubuntu* means becoming more fully human through deeper relationships with other human beings. It is because of this understanding that Enslin and Horsthemke (2004, p. 25) have argued that *ubuntu* is by definition speciesist and therefore cannot contribute positively towards addressing environmental problems. Through a categorical lens of environmental ethics they would say that *ubuntu* is anthropocentric. I wish to argue that this is not the case and that *ubuntu* has very strong ecocentric leanings (if the categorical lens of environmental ethics is used). To appreciate the ecocentric leanings of the concept *ubuntu* a broader concept, *ukama*, of which it forms part, should be understood. It is to the concept *ukama* that I now will turn. But before doing so a clarification is needed.

Like Metz and Gaie's exposition (2010), my discussion of *ubuntu* and moral obligation, 'should not be taken to represent anthropologically the beliefs of Africans about the right way to live' (p. 277). It is rather a theoretical reconstruction of themes that circulate in discourses in Africa south of the Sahara. However, unlike Metz and Gaie (2010), who do not discuss widespread beliefs among Africans about the existence of ancestors and their interactions with us, because they might be 'beyond the pale' of non-African scholars, I shall touch on this dimension only in so far as it strengthens my argument that *ubuntu* is not by definition anthropocentric.

Ukama and *ubuntu*

In the Shona[3] language there is a broader concept than *ubuntu*, *ukama*, which means relatedness—relatedness to the entire cosmos. Murove (2009) argues that *ubuntu* (humanness) is the concrete form of *ukama* (relatedness) in the sense that 'human interrelationship within society is a microcosm of the relationality within the universe' (p. 316). *Ukama* is the ChiShona version of the Zulu/Xhosa concept *buntu*. In Setswana (Bantu language belonging to the Niger–Congo family spoken in southern Africa) it is called *lesika*, and *letshinga* in Ikalanga (Bantu language spoken by people in Botswana and Zimbabwe).

Murove (2009, p. 316) points out that etymologically *ukama* is an adjective constructed *u-kama*—*u-* is an adjectival prefix and *-kama* an adjectival stem. *Kama* is a verb meaning to milk a cow or goat, and in Shona the idea of milking suggests closeness and affection. For example, *kama* results in affection because the one milking gets a benefit which can be shared by the community. Importantly, the milked animals are connected to the ancestors, so the exercise of milking links the animals and the person doing the milking to his/her relatives. Furthermore, those that are related by blood or marriage are *hama* which is a noun (Dale, 1994, p. 127). However, in Shona the meaning of *ukama* is not restricted to marital and blood ties (Murove, 2009, p. 316). The meaning of *ukama* extends to ties with all people, not only with present generations but also with past and future generations. Gelfand (1973) notes that the concept of 'brotherhood' (humanhood) and inseparable oneness with the ancestors are brought about through ritual practices of the Shona religion. He points out that *ukama* is an articulation of anamnestic solidarity because a person 'owes his [*sic*] personality and character to his *mudzimu* (ancestor)' (Gelfand, 1981, p. 8). The immortality of values through anamnesis is neatly captured by Bujo (2001, pp. 56–57):

> African ethics is articulated in the framework of anamnesis, which involves remembering one's ancestors. As a narrative community, fellowship here on earth renews the existence of the community of the ancestors. This re-establishing (poeisis) in turn implies the praxis which efficiently continues the remembrance of the ancestors and gives a new dynamism to the earthly fellowship. Consequently, ethical behaviour in the Black African context always involves re-establishing the presence of one's ancestors; for one who takes the anamnesis seriously is challenged to confront the ethical rules drawn up by the ancestors, in order to actualise anew the 'protological foundational act' which first called the clan (sic) fellowship into life.

Murove (2009, p. 319) adds that through anamnesis, 'human actions are sensitised to all dimensions of existence—past, present and future' and that 'the connecting thread in all three dimensions of existence is the moral values that have been inherited, treasured and passed on to future generations'. In short, the concept *ukama* embodies an inseparable oneness between past, present and future generations. However, *ukama* also means humanity's relatedness to the natural (biophysical) world, which is advanced through totemic ancestorhood. Junod (1939, p. 112), who conducted ethnological studies of baPedi, aptly notes:

> Totemism shows well one characteristic of the Bantu mind: the strong tendency to give a human soul to animals, to plants, to nature as such, a tendency which is at the very root of the most beautiful blossoms of poetry, a feeling that there is a community of substance between various forms of life.

It is against this backdrop that Murove's (2009, p. 317) assertion that, 'ukama provides the ethical anchorage for human social, spiritual and ecological togetherness', might be understood. This idea of ecological togetherness is supported by others such as Bujo (1998, pp. 22–23) who writes: 'The African is convinced that all things in the cosmos are interconnected.' Also by Tangwa (2004, p. 389) who avers: 'The precolonial traditional African metaphysical, outlook … impl[ies] recognition and acceptance of interdependence and peaceful coexistence between earth, plants, animals and humans.' And Opoka (1993, p.77) who notes: 'There is community with nature since man [*sic*] is part of nature and is expected to cooperate with it; and this sense of community with nature is often expressed in terms of identity and kinship, friendliness and respect.'

Moreover, the idea of the oneness of humans with nature expressed in Arne Naess's (1973) deep ecology, and the notion of wholeness of the earth expressed in James Lovelock's Gainism (1995) might have resided among African people for many centuries through notions such as *ukama*. As noted, *ubuntu* (humanness) is a concrete expression of *ukama*, that is, humanness needs to be understood relationally. In other words, humanness is an expression of interconnectedness between people and between people and the biophysical world. Moreover, humanness is not humanism and is in fact antithetical to it. As Ramose (2009, pp. 308–309) writes:

> Humanness suggests both a condition of being and the state of becoming, of openness or ceaseless unfolding. It is thus opposed to any, '-ism', including humanism, for this tends to suggest a condition of finality, a closedness or a kind of absolute either incapable of, or resistant to, any further movement.

Humanness is therefore inextricably bound up in the human being's connectedness with other human beings and with an ever-changing and complex (biophysical) world. In other words, *ubuntu* involves 'coming into presence' (Biesta, 2006, p. 9) of self in a changing social and biophysical world. The sense of wholeness and interconnectedness of self with the social and natural by implication means that caring for others also involves a duty to care for nature. *Ubuntu*, therefore, is not by definition speciesist as Enslin (2004, p. 25) suggests, but is rather an ecosophy that connects Guattari's (2001) three ecologies; self, social and nature—self, the social and nature are inextricably bound up with one another. Cultivating *ubuntu*, by definition, therefore involves healing of self, the social and nature.

Guattari's notion of transversality helps us to appreciate the notion of *ukama* when he argues that when suffering is witnessed in one ecological register it will also be witnessed in other ecological registers. Africa's suffering evident in the, 'staggering incidence of genocide, patriarchy, dictatorships and autocratic rule, corruption, sexism (and practices of genital excision), heterosexism and homophobia, and environmental degradation (and connected with this, human suffering) on the continent of Africa' (Horsthemke & Enslin, 2005, p. 67) should be understood as the breaking or erosion of *ukama* through, among other influences, years of colonial rule and apartheid–capitalism. Healing in one ecological register will therefore effect healing in other ecological dimensions. If *ubuntu* means that our deepest moral obligation is to become more fully human then this means not only fostering a closer and deeper relationship with human communities but also with biotic communities and the entire ecosphere. The realisation of one's true self cannot be achieved if other human beings and nature are exploited or harmed. *Ukama* as an expression of the connectedness to past and future generations also suggests a moral obligation to provide future generations with similar benefits to those that present generations are enjoying.

From the above discussion it is evident that there are two distinct claims about *ukama* and its implications for environmentalism. The first is that beliefs about ancestors entail a sense in which past, present and future generations are all part of the moral community. The second is that the fundamental relatedness of beings encapsulated by *ukama* includes a sense of relatedness with other natural entities, not just persons. The first claim is promising for an environmental ethic because environmental destruction (especially climate change) can potentially cause harm to many generations in the future. Relatedness to future generations as expressed in the notion of *ukama* can contribute to an ongoing discourse in environmental philosophy about our moral obligations to future generations. The second claim that *ukama* means relatedness to all natural entities is promising for an environmental ethic because relatedness to the entire natural world concerns caring for all of nature because it has intrinsic value—that nature needs to be cared for in the now/present.

Understanding *ubuntu* as a concrete expression of *ukama* also problematises the categories of anthropocentrism and ecocentrism (and those in between) which have come to characterise debates in environmental ethics/philosophy and rebounds on those who wish to impose such categories on African values such as *ubuntu*. Nurturing the self or caring for other human beings is not antagonistic towards caring for non-human nature—*ubuntu* cannot simply be reduced to a category of anthropocentric or ecocentric. The self, community and nature are inextricably bound up with one another—healing/development in one results in healing in all dimensions, so suffering, too, is transversally witnessed in all three dimensions. African spirituality cannot be reduced to a category of anthropocentric.

Implications for (moral) education

Given the deteriorating state of the environment (in all dimensions) it would be incumbent on a (moral) educator to make students aware of the causes of the degeneration of self, the social and nature so that they have an understanding of the (dis)connectedness among these dimensions. Metz and Gaie (2010, p. 280) argue that *ubuntu* entails that the goal of moral education should be to develop the personhood of students, which means facilitating their capacity to cherish community. They continue that this will lend weight to existing communal relationships and that it would be necessary for a moral educator to inform students of their responsibility not to upset norms central to a community's self-conception and that they should also engage in transmitting these values. However, they point out that it does not follow that moral education is a matter of ensuring that students mimic the past. They offer three reasons in support. Firstly, that knowledge should not be restricted to a fairly circumscribed culture given that even rural communities have to engage with a wide array of foreign people—solidarity with people cannot therefore be restricted to those comprising a local community. Secondly, that a moral educator ought not to rely on threats and rote regurgitation because truly sharing a way of life implies voluntary participation. Thirdly, because becoming a person includes caring about the quality of lives of others the moral educator should help students develop capacities for sympathy and encourage them to engage in helping others.

I support Metz and Gaie's (2010, p. 280) sentiments but wish to extend them. In the light of previous discussion, a moral education guided by *ubuntu* should not be restricted to facilitating students' capacity to cherish only human communities but non-human nature as well. Personhood cannot be developed independently of human communities and the natural world. Just as it is incumbent on the moral educator to inform students of their responsibility to not upset norms central to a community's self-conception so, too, the moral educator should inform students of their responsibility not to upset dynamic interactions between living and non-living components of ecosystems and not to contribute to breaking important links in food chains/webs. Moreover, students should be guided as to how to take action in the interest of both human and non-human communities. Just as students need to understand the responsibility to cultivate solidarities with all people, and more so now that they interact with those deemed to be foreign (different or other) because people migrate more easily across national boundaries, so, too, they need to understand their connectedness with the biosphere—that they also need to act in the interest of other species (different or other). However, charity does begin at home and part of the development of the personhood of the student would have to be about (re)connecting the student to place or places—that students should learn to know their local environments—the biotic communities including the names of plant and animal species and energy flows as living components interact with non-living components.

Furthermore, I agree that the moral educator should not simply be a dispenser of knowledge and an authority figure, nor should she just be a provider of experiences. Moral educators ought to be co-investigators with students and simultaneously a knowing adult. In other words the moral educator should be a resourceful person, organising critical and collaborative projects in negotiation with students and community. These projects may entail investigating environmental problems in local communities including what the moral responsibilities might be, so as to improve environmentally risky positions. It is through projects of this kind that the personhood of the students could develop, communities be strengthened and the environment cared for. In moral education students do not take on the role of passive receivers of knowledge but are active learners/investigators. Moral education guided by *ubuntu* cannot only entail teaching students about moral responsibility/obligation *vis-à-vis* human communities and the biophysical world. Doing so will teach students the lesson of hypocrisy—that it is sufficient to learn about moral responsibility without having to do anything. Providing learners with experiences in social and natural settings so that they can both clarify and choose values to adopt is also not an adequate approach. Moral education should involve the *enactment* of moral responsibility—getting students involved in actions for (in the interest of) human and non-human communities. Moreover, moral education guided by *ubuntu* is not so much concerned with the *essence* or nature of the human being but the *being* of the human being, how the human being *exists* in the world. A focus on what it means to be human could result in defining other humans as less human and other species as non-human and therefore inferior. Ramose (2009, p. 309) reminds us that *ubuntu* suggests both a condition of being and the state of becoming—the human being becomes present in interaction with communities and the biophysical world and acts in the social and natural world by caring for these.

How might all of this be realised in formal education? Are there opportunities for a moral education guided by *ubuntu* in formal schooling? I shall briefly attempt to respond to these questions by referring to education in South Africa.

Post-apartheid curriculum policy in South Africa mandates that both indigenous knowledge and environmental concerns be integrated into all school learning areas/subjects.[4] One of the principles on which the National Curriculum Statement (NCS) for Further Education and Training (FET) is based is 'valuing indigenous knowledge systems' (SA. DoE, 2003, p. 4). Another principle is the promotion of 'human rights, inclusivity, environmental and social justice' (SA. DoE, 2003, p. 4). The former principle is elaborated as follows: 'Indigenous knowledge systems in the South African context refers to a body of knowledge embedded in African philosophical thinking and social practices that have evolved over thousands of years.' Furthermore, the 10 values[5] identified in South Africa's *Manifesto on values, education and democracy* (SA. DoE, 2001) are purported to find expression in both the General Education and Training (GET) and FET curriculum statements. One of the 10 values is *ubuntu* (human dignity). Evidently, African philosophical thinking generally, and *ubuntu* more specifically, are central features of post-apartheid curriculum frameworks. The inclusion of values such as *ubuntu* is intended to restore, through education, values that have become eroded as a consequence of centuries of colonialism and decades of apartheid. The basis for a moral education guided by *ubuntu* is therefore supported by the curriculum intended for South African schools. The extent to which the curriculum intended might be manifested in school classrooms would depend on the role that the (moral) educator plays, as described earlier. But, who might the moral educator be? Presumably, it could be an educator teaching any learning area/subject—it certainly would be ideal if all teachers could be moral educators in the mould discussed in this paper. However, one learning area/subject Life Orientation offers opportunities for a moral education of the kind described. This is evident in the purpose of the learning area/subject described below:

> The Life Orientation Learning Area aims to empower learners to use their talents to achieve their full physical, intellectual, personal, emotional and social potential. Learners will develop the skills to relate positively and make a contribution to family, community and society, while practising the values embedded in the Constitution ... The Life Orientation Learning Area will enable learners to make informed, morally responsible and accountable decisions about health and the environment. (SA. DoE, 2002, p. 4)

Life Orientation is a compulsory subject for all South African school learners, taken from Grade R (age 6) through to Grade 12 (age 18). Unfortunately, because the subject carries fewer credits than other subjects it tends to be neglected and given to any teacher to teach so as to make up their required teaching loads. The point, though, is that the opportunity for moral education guided by *ubuntu* does exist in formal education in South Africa and can be realised should appropriate moral educators be tasked with the responsibility.

Conclusion

A recurrent theme which has characterised debates in environmental theory/philosophy is the anthropocentric–ecocentric distinction. I begin the article by clarifying terms such as anthropocentric and ecocentrism (as well as related terms). I do this because some such as Enslin and Horsthemke (2004, p. 25) have argued that *ubuntu* is by definition speciesist and therefore cannot contribute positively towards addressing environmental problems. I argue that *ubuntu* needs to be understood as a microcosm of (or concrete expression of) a broader concept *ukama*, which means relatedness—relatedness to the entire cosmos. Understood in this way, *ubuntu* is not only concerned about the development of the self in an individualistic way, but that the development of the true self is inextricably bound up in relationships with other humans and non-human nature. I then use this understanding of *ubuntu* to map out what a moral education guided by *ubuntu* might entail through extending the work of Metz and Gaie (2010). I briefly explore opportunities that post-apartheid national curriculum frameworks provide for enacting a moral education of this kind.

Moral education ought to be concerned with how the young come into presence as beings so as to take responsibility for the world, or as Arendt (1954, p. 193) put it, 'to love the world enough to assume responsibility for it'. *Ubuntu* is at the heart of such an idea of (moral) education, because it concerns a condition of being that becomes/unfolds in relationship with the other (other human beings and the biophysical world).

Acknowledgements

I thank the anonymous reviewers for offering helpful comments on an earlier version of this paper.

Notes

1. In this article I shall use the term *ubuntu* which derives from the aphorism '*Umuntu ngumuntu ngabantu*' found in the Nguni languages of Zulu, Xhosa or Ndebele. However, I wish to point out that a similar concept exists in Sotho-Tswana languages derived from the proverbial expression, '*Motho ke motho ka batho babang*' [a person is a person because of other people].
2. The Xhosa people are Bantu language speakers living in the south-east of South Africa. The main tribes of the Xhosa are: Mpondo, Mpondomise, Bonvana, Xesibe and Thembu. isiXhosa is one of the official languages of South Africa.
3. Shona is the collective name for several groups of people in the east of Zimbabwe and southern Mozambique. The Shona-speaking people are categorised into five main ethnic groups: Zezuru, Manyika, Karanga and Kalanga, Korekore and Ndau. There are substantial numbers in South Africa and Botswana.
4. In the South African education system the term 'learning area' is used in the General Education and Training (GET) band and the term 'subject' in the Further Education and Training (FET) band.
5. The 10 values in the *Manifesto on values, education and democracy* are: democracy, social justice and equity, non-racism and non-sexism, *ubuntu* (human dignity), an open society, accountability (responsibility), respect, the rule of law, reconciliation.

References

Arendt, H. (1954). *Between past and future*. New York: Penguin Group.

Barry, J., & Eckersley, R. (Eds.). (2005). *The state of the global ecological crisis*. Cambridge, MA: MIT Press.

Battle, M. (1996). The ubuntu theology of Desmond Tutu. In L. Hulley, L. Kretzschmar, & L. Lungile (Eds.), *Archbishop Tutu: Prophetic witness in South Africa*. Cape Town: Human & Rousseau.

Beck, U. (1992). *Risk society: Towards a new modernity*. New York: Sage Publications.

Biesta, G. (2006). *Beyond learning: Democratic education for a human future*. London: Paradigm Publishers.

Bowers, C.A., & Apffel-Marglin, F. (Eds.). (2005). *Rethinking Freire: Globalization and the environmental crisis*. Mahway, NJ: Lawrence Erlbaum Associates.

Bujo, B. (1998). *The ethical dimension of community*. Nairobi: Paulines Publications.

Bujo, B. (2001). *Foundations of an African ethic: Beyond the universal claims of Western morality*. New York: The Crossroad Publishing Company.

Carson, R. (1962). *The silent spring*. Boston, MA: Houghton-Mifflin.

Dale, D. (1994). *A basic English–Shona dictionary*. Gweru: Mambo Press.

Ehrlich, P., & Ehrlich, A. (1970). *Population, resources, environment: Issues in human ecology*. San Francisco, CA: Freeman.

Enslin, P., & Horsthemke, K. (2004). Can ubuntu provide a model for citizenship education in African democracies? Proceedings of the 9th biennial conference of the International Network of Philosophers of Education, 4–7 August 2004, Universidad Complutense, Madrid.

Gelfand, M. (1973). *The genuine Shona: Survival values of an African culture*. Gweru: Mambo Press.

Gelfand, M. (1981). *Ukama, reflections on Shona and Western cultures in Zimbabwe*. Gweru: Mambo Press.

Guattari, F. (2001) *The three ecologies*, Trans. I. Pindar & P. Sutton. London: The Athlone Press.

Horsthemke, K., & Enslin, P. (2005). Is there a distinctively and uniquely African philosophy of education. In Y. Waghid (Ed.), *African(a) philosophy of education: Reconstructions and deconstructions*. Stellenbosch: Department of Education Policy Studies.

Janse van Rensburg, E. (1994). Social transformation in response to the environmental crisis: The role of education and research. *Australian Journal of Environmental Education, 10*, 1–20.

Junod, P. (1939). *Bantu heritage*. Johannesburg: Hortors Limited.

Le Roux, J. (2000). The concept of '*ubuntu*': Africa's most important contribution to multicultural education? *Multicultural Teaching, 18*(2), 43–46.

Lovelock, J. (1995). *Gaia: A new look at life on earth*. Oxford: Oxford University Press.

Meadows, D.H., Meadows, D.L., Randers, J., & Behrens, M. (1974). *The limits to growth*. London: Pan Books.

Metz, T., & Gaie, J.B.R. (2010). The African ethic of Ubuntu/Botho: Implications for research on morality. *Journal of Moral Education, 39*(3), 273–290.

Murove, M.F. (2009). An African environmental ethic based on the concepts of ukama and ubuntu. In M.F. Murove (Ed.), *African ethics: An anthology of comparative and applied ethics*. Pietermaritzburg: University of Kwazulu-Natal Press.

Naess, A. (1984). A defence of the deep ecology movement. *Environmental Ethics, 6*, 265–270.

Opoka, K. (1993). African traditional religion: An enduring heritage. In J. Olupona & S. Nyang (Eds.), *Religious plurality in Africa*. Berlin: Mouton de Gruyter.

Ramose, M.B. (2009). Ecology through ubuntu. In M.F. Murove (Ed.), *African ethics: An anthology of comparative and applied ethics*. Pietermaritzburg: University of KwaZulu-Natal Press.

Schreuder, D. (1995). Delusions of progress: A case of reconceptualising environmental education. *Southern African Journal of Environmental Education, 15*, 18–25.

South Africa. Department of Education (SA. DoE). (2001). *Manifesto on values, education and democracy*. Pretoria: Department of Education.

South Africa. Department of Education (SA. DoE). (2002). *Revised national curriculum statement grades R-9 (schools) Life Orientation*. Pretoria: Department of Education.

South Africa. Department of Education (SA. DoE). (2003). *National curriculum statement grades 10–12 (general) Life Sciences*. Pretoria: Department of Education.

Tangwa, G. (2004). Some African reflections on biomedical and environmental ethics. In K. Wiredu (Ed.), *A companion to African philosophy*. Malden, MA: Blackwell.

Venter, E. (2004). The notion of ubuntu and communalism in African educational discourse. *Studies in Philosophy and Education, 23*(2–3), 149–160.

Some implications for moral education of the Confucian principle of harmony: learning from sustainability education practice in China

Ling Feng[a] and Derek Newton[b]
[a]*Chinese Academy of Personnel Science, P. R. China;* [b]*Huddersfield University, UK*

The concept of 'harmony' was taught by the Chinese sages as the practice of acceptance, tolerance, mutual respect, equality and patience, and is now given great importance by the Chinese government in its attempts to promote the stability and sustainability of the country. The concept could have significant implications for moral education. This article uses a Chinese Masters course on sustainability education as an example to analyse the positive and negative implications of the principle of harmony both for the practice of sustainability education and for educational practice in general. The course encouraged students to plan and implement feasible and practical sustainability activities mainly in the context of Chinese schools. Influenced by the value of harmony, the course chose to promote sustainability in a pragmatic but limited way. Although the course resulted in some practical sustainability related activities, a holistic and critical view on sustainability was not evident amongst the students. However, the principle of harmony could be applied critically both as a criterion for evaluating social development and as a value underlying democratic decision-making.

Introduction

Yu Tzu said, 'Of the things brought about by the rites, harmony is the most valuable. Of the ways of the Former Kings, this is the most beautiful, and is followed alike in matters great and small, yet this will not always work: to aim always at harmony without regulating it by the rites simply because one knows only about harmony will not, in fact, work' (Confucius, *The analects*,[1] Book 1.12).

The Confucian concept of 'harmony' (*he xie*) has deeply influenced Chinese culture and the ways in which Chinese ideas about morality and education are constructed. In China, the boundaries between 'social, interpersonal values (morality) and political values (ideology)' are less clearly defined than in some Western ethical discourses (Li, Zhong, Lin, & Zhang, 2004). This can be seen as a direct legacy of the Confucian tradition in which social harmony is seen as the highest moral ideal and, therefore, a goal of personal conduct; harmony is the core value in Confucianism, which is, itself, regarded as symbolic of Chinese culture (Li, 2011). At a practical level, the value placed on harmony can be interpreted as a preference for compromise over conflict, reform over revolution and eclecticism over dogma. In its emphasis on consensus and pragmatism, historically, this Confucian influence has enabled Chinese people to act cooperatively and to accomplish significant collective projects. On the other hand, it has sometimes acted as a barrier to critical thinking, in effect, acting as a form of internal censorship. Influenced by Confucianism, Chinese students are brought up to respect, rather than challenge, those who provide knowledge (Chan, 1999).

In this article we try to illustrate these two facets of 'consensual thinking' by taking examples from a Chinese Masters course on sustainability education, and showing how the dominance of the concept of harmony can have both positive and negative implications for moral thought. We examine the significance this may have for the formulation of meaningful responses to the socio-environmental challenges facing China (and the world). We try to draw out some differences in the ways that controversy and critique are understood and handled in Chinese educational contexts compared with Western educational contexts, recognising that although these differences are real, they should not be understood as either absolute or essential.

Sustainability education and moral education

This article uses the term 'sustainability education' as a generic and inclusive title that can accommodate differing interpretations including environmental education, education for sustainable development (ESD) and education for sustainability (EfS), etc., but we are aware of other conceptualisations underpinning different and more specific terms. Sustainability education may be seen as affiliated to moral education in its concern with values and value systems. Jickling (2009) calls attention to the 'rich bodies of literature and practice' associated with environmental ethics. Indeed, as Dale and Newman (2005) have pointed out, sustainability education has sometimes been criticised as being 'overly value-based'.

One example may serve to illustrate this close relationship between sustainability education and moral education. In 2005, as part of the United Nations Decade of Education for Sustainable Development (2005–2014), the United Nations Educational, Scientific and Cultural Organisation (UNESCO) published a report, *Guidelines and recommendations for reorienting teacher education to address sustainability*, which states explicitly:

> Values are also an integral part of ESD. In some cultures, values are taught overtly in the schools. In other cultures, however, even if values are not overtly taught, they are modelled, explained, analysed, or discussed. In both situations, understanding values is an essential part of understanding your own worldview and other people's viewpoints. Understanding your own values, the values of the society you live in, and the values of

> others around the world is a central part of educating for a sustainable future. (UNESCO, 2005, p. 73)

The report recommends that student teachers should be given 'opportunities to explore their own values and attitudes towards local sustainability problems and those of the surrounding region' (UNESCO, 2005, p. 44).

However, this emphasis on the ethical dimension of sustainability education is far from being unproblematic. In particular, there has been opposition to the idea that sustainability education should promote 'a new, socio-environmental ethic', as advocated by one of the contributors to the UNESCO report (2005, p. 27). For example, Dale and Newman (2005) cite Jickling's view that placing the values of sustainability and sustainable development as 'desired outcomes' of education is tantamount to indoctrination. Foster (2005) has discussed and elucidated at some length what he sees as the complexity and uncertainty surrounding 'environmental values', arguing that uncertainty in this area is '*in principle irresolvable.* Present actions, including those involved in representing future environmental values to ourselves, inevitably shape the future values which we are trying to anticipate' (p. 117).

Western concepts of academic freedom, with their emphasis on moral and intellectual independence from external authority, allied to a typically individualist epistemology, tend to problematise the relationship between scholarly activity and social (and especially political) action (Palfreyman, 2007). Foster, in particular, has argued for the commonly accepted liberal view that sees education as 'radically non-instrumental: an end in itself' (2001, p. 164). Education, and especially higher education, should not be subservient to what he calls an operational or socio-scientific concept of sustainability, i.e. a definable 'set of guidelines and constraints for collective and individual decision making' (Foster, 2001, p. 156). Rather, *operational sustainability* should be superseded by *deep sustainability*, which is 'not a measurable condition or trend, but a particular way of being humanly alert to and alive through the world' (Foster, 2001, p. 160). Deep sustainability requires the nurturing of a *learning mind-set*, 'a positive, eager commitment to the heuristic creativity of intelligence in encountering each emergent tomorrow' (Foster, 2001, p. 161). Dale and Newman have expressed this argument somewhat more straightforwardly, suggesting that sustainability education should be process-based rather than goal-oriented, meaning that students should be encouraged to reflect critically 'on competing definitions of sustainable development and the values that underlie them'. In their view, the role of sustainability education is to enable students to articulate values and acquire 'techniques to reach consensus among varying value systems' (Dale & Newman, 2005, p. 354). We would argue that this positioning of students as reflective critics serves to legitimate an approach to teaching and learning in which a plurality of views, including those that are controversial, can be expressed and examined without seeming to violate the ethical and intellectual autonomy attributed to the learner. Whether this autonomy is more apparent than real is a moot point.

The value of harmony in Chinese culture

Confucianism originated around 2500 years ago and was established as the orthodox basis of moral education in China during the Han dynasty (206 BC to 220 CE). Its formulations of pragmatic rules for daily life are seen as being derived from the lessons of Chinese history. Although (or perhaps because) Confucius' teachings are unsystematic and frequently ambiguous, they have been studied intensively for their lessons in practical ethics. As a whole, Confucianism presents a range of precepts regarding the role and appropriate forms of behaviour associated with the different members of Chinese society, public and private, governing and governed. In fact, these kinds of distinctions do not properly exist in Confucian thought since private morality is simultaneously a public good. Confucianism proposes that all rulers must govern with benevolence and justice and that people must obey and respect their leaders in return. This 'obedience', however, is rooted in the moral character of individuals and their understanding of what is right and proper, rather than in submission to direct commands. 'The end of [Confucianist] education is to guide people to pursue moral perfection in realising the life that performs goodness and benevolence' (Jin & Dan, 2004, p. 576).

Froese (2008, p. 261) argues that Confucian philosophy is premised on a 'prominent cosmological assumption ... that there is a harmony in nature that emerges spontaneously', and is manifest in the cycle of nature and the abundance of natural generation.

> The Master said, 'What does Heaven ever say? Yet there are the four seasons going round and there are the hundred things coming into being. What does Heaven ever say?' (*The analects*, 17.19)

The Chinese term, *tian*, usually translated as 'heaven', might more properly be considered as a cosmic principle that informs and unites both the natural and the human order. In Chinese *tian* is sometimes regarded as a synonym for *tiandi*, heaven *and* earth. The cosmic principle does not reveal itself (speak) directly and yet it does reveal itself (speak). Froese (2008) argues that the division between nature and culture that characterises Western thought is absent from Confucianism. Rather, through ritual, people are able to 'participate in the meaningful order of *tian*' (Froese, 2008, p. 261). Ritual, in this context, should be understood as comprising not only religious ceremonial but also that decorous and respectful behaviour towards others that each person is expected to practise, first within the family then within an ever-extending web of relationships. The family is both an instance of and a metaphor for the wider human community, including the state. Human community, then, is the site in which it is possible for people to cultivate harmonious relationships consistent with the cosmic principle.

At first sight Confucianist ethics seem prescriptive, and whilst they affirm moral responsibility, they seem to deny ethical autonomy. However, Huang (2011, p. 147) argues that 'for Confucius, the goal of moral education is not to issue moral commands but to stimulate a person's moral sentiments'. He translates *The analects*

17.9, in which Confucius discusses the study of classical poetry, as saying that poetry 'can serve to stimulate one's imagination, sharpen one's sensitivity, increase one's sense of solidarity'. Moreover, *The analects* 13.23 states: 'The gentleman agrees with others (seeks harmony) without being an echo. The small man echoes without being in agreement.' This seems to imply that agreement (harmony) is not a mere formality but a relationship that must be entered into willingly, with understanding and in the right spirit. There are many places in *The analects* where Confucius criticises mere eloquence and argues for the priority of deeds over fine words. To give just one example, *The analects* 4.22 says: 'In antiquity men were loath to speak. This was because they counted it shameful if their person failed to keep up with their words.' Speech should be trustworthy and sincere; people should be slow to speak but quick to act. Huang argues that for Confucius 'what non-virtuous persons lack is not an intellectual understanding of virtue but the sentiment or desire to be virtuous, it is important to stimulate such a sentiment or desire in them' (Huang, 2011, p. 153). The key to promoting virtue (and, thus, harmony) is personal example: 'When the gentleman feels profound affection for his parents, the common people will be stirred to benevolence. When he does not forget friends of long standing, the common people will not shirk their obligations to other people' (*The analects* 8.2).

It is widely held by Chinese scholars that, although the Confucian 'principle of harmony' may sometimes have delayed or prevented necessary reforms due to its apparently conservative nature, it has, equally, played a positive role in the country's resilience and development for two millennia (D.C. Li, 2010; Z.G. Li, 2011). This emphasis on the value of harmony is not merely a tradition from the past, but something that holds a prominent and increasingly influential position in contemporary China. Following the Cultural Revolution, Confucian moral teachings, with their emphasis on social responsibility, were rehabilitated, initially under the auspices of so-called 'neo-conservatives' (Lee & Ho, 2005). More recently, China's political leaders have seen a return to China's ancient cultural roots as a means of resolving conflicts that have emerged in today's complex modern society (Fung, 2006). In 2005, Chinese President Hu Jintao instructed the country's leading officials and Party cadres to place 'building a harmonious society' at the top of their agenda. In a harmonious society, it is argued, the political environment is stable, the economy is prosperous, people live in peace and work in comfort, and social welfare improves (Li, 2010). This is a direct echo of *The analects* 16.1: 'For where there is even distribution there is no such thing as poverty, where there is harmony there is no such thing as underpopulation and where there is stability there is no such thing as overturning.'

Case study

In 2009, the first author carried out a case study of a Masters course in sustainability education in China. The aim of the case study was to identify the key characteristics of the course and to analyse the participants' experiences of and perspectives on the course. The case study was mainly conducted through documentary analysis and interviews. The students were mostly in-service school teachers. The two-year course, which could be taken by part-time study only, was designed to meet their needs and interests. The main content included the design, implementation, evaluation and management of sustainability-related curriculum activities and projects in the school context. The aim stated in the course publication was 'to enhance the theoretical understanding and practice of sustainable development educators, so that they can carry out sustainability education in a better way and promote sustainable development' (Course publication, 2005, p. 34).

The course was the first and, so far, the only degree course in sustainability education in China. It started in 2004, originating from an international conference on sustainability education in 2003. During the conference, the course director had advised the conference organisers that a few scholars attending conferences were not sufficient to move things forward—sustainability education in China needed 'doers' and actions needed to be concrete. Soon after the conference, a partnership aimed at establishing the course was formed between a government educational institute and the university where the course director worked.

One of the key characteristics of the course was its direct and practical approach towards encouraging students' sustainability education activity in their workplace. The course director believed that in-service school staff play the most important role in promoting sustainability education in practice:

> The aim of establishing the course is to develop human resources, i.e. teachers. They are the main force for promoting sustainability education in China. ... I told the students, I see you like seeds, you need to germinate and flower and fructify in the future.

When the students were interviewed, they also endorsed the practice-based focus of the curriculum. As one of the students said:

> Sustainability education in the district should be promoted through us—the students. We should take the leadership in promoting sustainability education in the district in the future ... you have to study well to be able to make a difference.[2]

It was clear from student interviews and questionnaires that one of the tutors was particularly popular because of the practice-based focus of her teaching. Her sessions were full of examples from her rich experience as a practitioner.

> I oriented my session on practice. For example, the students saw my teaching plans, saw the essays supervised by me, saw project proposals sent for a competition, all very practical. ... Although I am not a big expert, I am an observer and a practitioner, so I can use what I've observed, what I've done and what I've tried to communicate with people, which is no weaker than the experts' big theories. ... Be practical and realistic.

One of the students explained: 'why she impressed people, the most crucial reason is that she is a practitioner, a successful practitioner. She has done so well. We should learn from her'.

This emphasis on the value of practical experience over theoretical knowledge was also apparent in the students' comments on another tutor whose sessions were also highly appreciated.

> He has been at the front line. Instead of standing high above the masses, only researching on big theories, he has been to all the sustainability education experimental schools. I think many researchers who did big projects, national projects, they have not talked to the front line teachers. As a result, their findings were completely useless for schools.

The tutor encouraged the students to talk about their problems in practice and gave them feedback. Another student told me:

> From theory to practice, he gave you methodological guidance. We studied the theory, we also know the methods, know how to implement this, what I can do, I felt my thirst was satisfied this way. After listening to him, 'this makes sense, I will go back and try it, I should do it like this'. Many people feel like this.

One student was so enthused that he started putting into practice what he learnt on the course almost immediately:

> You see, I started to study the course in October 2004. At the end of 2004, I started to organise the teachers [in his school] to do learning organisation development. ... Whatever I thought was important in the course, I passed it on to our staff afterwards, also modified according to our educational practice. ... Some of our staff members' level exceeded the course students' level, because we learned and practised at the same time, gained understanding as well as practical experience [in our school].

The students' practical application of their learning mainly took the form of what might be regarded as conventional sustainability activities and projects such as recycling, energy-saving and handicrafts, or involved integrating sustainability concepts, such as ecological and cultural diversity, into the wider curriculum.

Commentary

Although the course included modules in which theoretical perspectives on sustainable development and sustainability education were explored, it was apparent from the interviews that the students had little interest in problem-(re)defining and did not see it as a crucial step before taking action. In this respect, perhaps, Chinese teachers are not so different from their eclectic and pragmatic colleagues in other parts of the world. However, although this ethos and approach efficiently stimulated and spread sustainability education activities and projects in the short term, it lacked the capacity to develop a framework or frameworks for engaging with more fundamental questions about sustainability. In our view, what was also needed was the ability to generate more critical, in-depth and wide-ranging perspectives with possibly longer-term outcomes.

In part, this reflects a reluctance among Chinese teachers to engage publicly in overtly political debate. For example, one student described an incident when the students and a tutor chose to foreclose a discussion: it was a session on the background of sustainability education. Somehow, a few students started to talk about the government's roles in promoting sustainability. The discussion quickly turned to complaints about the government's inability to do so and problems with the political and economic system. What was striking was that the student said that she felt the discussion was completely irrelevant to the session. She had asked those students to stop the discussion and come back to the session's main theme. The tutor and quite a few other students agreed with her and the discussion did stop, thereby foreclosing a discussion that was potentially important but which might have ended in 'disharmony'.

Implications of the principle of harmony for Chinese sustainability education practice

What the course promoted—consensual thinking and the identification and undertaking of practical sustainability activities—contrasts in important ways with the position discussed earlier in which the learner was characterised as an individual and reflective critic capable of reconciling disparate value systems. Whilst some features of the case study course were particular and contingent, we believe that it is useful to interpret some of its key characteristics in terms of the Confucian heritage, with its emphasis on community values, on deeds rather than words and on the moral value of personal example. It can be argued that the case study illustrates the way in which the principle of harmony both promotes effective action, potentially leading to change, yet, at the same time, tends to limit its scope. The principal value of consensual thinking is that it prompts people to define those issues on which they can agree and allows them to act cooperatively in order to achieve a common, albeit limited, agenda. In other words, consensual thinking facilitates cooperative action. On the other hand, the desire for harmony and cooperative activity can discourage critical thinking, since critical thinking might challenge the validity of the agreed agenda and lead to the proposed course of action being indefinitely postponed. We would suggest that reference to the principle of harmony and, by implication, the Confucian moral framework in which it is rooted, invokes the possibility of negotiating the simultaneous yet contradictory demands for social change and social stability.

The experience of the Cultural Revolution and the break up of the Soviet Union have made the Chinese political leadership very wary of radical social and political transformation (Jia, 2009). Many ordinary Chinese citizens fear the chaos and violence that might accompany political change. Whilst wanting to participate in and contribute to the 'progress' that Chinese society seems to be experiencing, they are cautious about advocating ideas that might threaten stability or appear to challenge the status quo (Kang, 2002). The crucial question facing China is whether, as the country with the second largest population in poverty in the world, it can effect any significant transformation without inadvertently increasing human misery on a monumental scale; or, as the Chinese political leadership sees it—social stability is the definite precondition of development.

By their nature, sustainability issues are hugely complicated and highly political. The current, unsustainable forms of development are deeply rooted in problematic social, economic and political systems. It is widely accepted in the West that sustainability education needs to recognise the limitations of technological fixes and information-based consciousness-raising, and apply a critical thinking approach that resists ready-made description and interpretations, or routine and unresponsive behaviour (Parker, 1997). However, some versions of sustainability education are deeply inimical to any form of implied collectivism: *operational sustainability* 'tends to demote the individual life-project in this way—since a concept making essential reference to general welfare and to ecosytemic resources as public goods can, of course, only be predicated of collectivities' (Foster, 2001, p. 162). On the other hand, socially critical sustainability educators have encouraged learners to recognise and face up to 'the role of power relations in the formation of knowledge about the ecosocial crisis' and to engage with 'the political forces that shape their lives' (Plant, 2001, p. 164). Gough (1997) compares the famous 'three Rs: reduce, re-use, recycle' with her socially critical three Rs: 'refusal, reconstruction, redirection', claiming that, unless sustainability education adopts a radical political perspective it 'neglects to look at the broader social issues' and thus, is 'tenuous and grossly ineffective' despite international efforts (p. 154).

In conclusion

As argued above, the concept of harmony resonates deeply among people who are steeped, albeit unconsciously, in the traditions of Confucian thought. It is also embedded in many underlying conceptions of sustainability. With its emphasis on pragmatism and consensus, this principle can facilitate collective and cooperative forms of action, based on respect for others and recognition of mutual interests. Indeed, at its core, the Confucian principle of harmony implies that respect for others *is* a mutual interest. The question arises whether this set of values and the discourses in which they are situated are inherently conservative and, therefore, incapable of rising to the unprecedented environmental and social challenges China is facing, given its large population, low per-capita resources, fragile ecosystem, uneven regional economic development and underdeveloped social security system. As we have suggested, the principle of harmony can promote activities directed towards addressing sustainability issues, but may significantly and damagingly limit their scope. On the other hand, might it not be possible to employ the concept of harmony to examine in a more radical way the conditions that act as barriers to the creation of a sustainable and harmonious society? In its identification of corruption as the major threat to social harmony, the Chinese government has, in some respects, already opened up this possibility.

The Chinese government wishes education to play a leading role in building a country capable of innovation. For it to do so, Chinese education needs to promote transformative learning and break with its currently dominant, transmissive, forms of educational discourse and practice. Transmissive learning takes place within pre-established boundaries, focusing on information and leaving basic values unexamined (Sterling, 2010); whereas transformative learning encourages innovation beyond the boundaries through the practice of fair and participatory decision-making and collective action (Fien & Gough, 1996). It is this aspect of the concept of harmony, i.e. the way in which it could promote participatory decision-making and collective action, which might enable it to emerge, not as a barrier to critical thinking, but as a powerful force for engaging and mobilising Chinese learners within the movement towards creating a sustainable future.

The core of the Confucian idea of 'harmony', with its emphasis on mutual respect rooted in the moral character of individuals rather than in external authority, is a powerful ethical principle that is worthy of deeper consideration in the context of moral education. The example we have given indicates that this principle can give rise to cooperative forms of behaviour that can act powerfully for the public good. As we have suggested, interpreted in a conservative way, the principle of harmony can act as a barrier to critical thinking. However, we believe that it can also be deployed in ways that enable us to address some of the fundamental issues that face us today, how to live together in ways that are sustainable and of benefit to all.

Notes

1. In researching this article we have consulted three English-language translations of *The analects*: Ames R.T. & Rosemont, H. Jr. (1999). *The analects of Confucius: A philosophical translation*. New York: Ballantine Books; Dawson, R. (2008). *Confucius: The analects*. Oxford: Oxford World's Classics; Lau, D.C. (1979). *Confucius: The analects*. London: Penguin Books. All quotations are based on the translation by D.C. Lau. In one case we have slightly amended the quotation to make the meaning clearer.
2. Quotations from the students were translated from Chinese by the first author.

References

Chan, S. (1999). The Chinese learner—A question of style. *Education and Training, 41*(6/7), 294–304.

Dale, A., & Newman, L. (2005). Sustainable development, education and literacy. *International Journal of Sustainability in Higher Education, 6*(4), 351–362.

Fien, J., & Gough, A. (1996). Environmental education. In R. Gilbert (Ed.), *Studying society and the environment: A handbook for teachers*. Melbourne: Macmillan Education Australia.

Foster, J. (2001). Education as sustainability. *Environmental Education Research, 7*(2), 153–165.

Foster, J. (2005). Options, sustainability policy and the spontaneous order. *Environmental Education Research, 11*(1), 115–135.

Froese, K. (2008). The art of becoming human: Morality in Kant and Confucius. *Dao: a Journal of Comparative Philosophy, 7*, 257–268.

Fung, F. (2006). *Chinese harmony and American democracy in the 21st century*. Available online at: http://news.xinhuanet.com/english/2006-11/01/content_5281331_1.htm (accessed 10 June 2011).

Gough, A. (1997). *Education and the environment: Policy, trends and the problem of maginalisation, Australian Education Review, N. 39.* Melbourne: Australian Council for Educational Research.

Huang, Y. (2011). Can virtue be taught and how? Confucius on the paradox of moral education. *Journal of Moral Education, 40*(2), 141–159.

Jia, Q.L. (2009). *Improving the multi-party cooperation and consultation system led by the Chinese Communist Party on the path of Chinese socialism.* Available online at: http://news.xinhuanet.com/politics/2009-11/01/content_12368043.htm (accessed 4 November 2009).

Jickling, B. (2009). Environmental education research: To what ends? *Environmental education research, 15*(2), 209–216.

Jin, S.H., & Dan, J.W. (2004). The contemporary development of philosophy of education in mainland China and Taiwan. *Comparative Education, 40*(4), 571–581.

Kang, X.G. (2002). Political stability of mainland China in the next 3 to 5 years. *Strategy and Management, 3,* 15–19.

Lee, W.O., & Ho, C.H. (2005). Ideopolitical shifts and changes in moral education policy in China. *Journal of Moral Education, 34*(4), 413–431.

Li, D.C. (2010). *Harmonious society's moral foundation.* Beijing: China Logistics Publishing House.

Li, P., Zhong, M., Lin, B., & Zhang, H. (2004). *Deyu* as moral education in modern China: ideological functions and transformations. *Journal of Moral Education, 33*(4), 449–464.

Li, Z.G. (2011). *Chuan tong yu xian dai zhi jian: zhong guo wen hua xian dai hua de zhe xue xing si* [Between the traditional and the modern: philosophical thinking on the modernisation of Chinese culture]. Beijing: Beijing Normal University.

Palfreyman, D. (2007). Is academic freedom under threat in UK and US higher education? *Education and the Law, 19*(1), 19–40.

Parker, S. (1997). *Reflective teaching in the postmodern world: A manifesto for education in postmodernity.* Buckingham: Open University Press.

Plant, M. (2001). Developing and evaluating a socially critical approach to Environmental Education at philosophical and methodological levels in higher education. Unpublished PhD thesis, Nottingham Trent University.

Sterling, S. (2010). Learning for resilience, or the resilient learner? Towards a necessary reconciliation in a paradigm of sustainable education. *Environmental Education Research, 16*(5), 511–528.

UNESCO. (2005). *Guidelines and recommendations for reorienting teacher education to address sustainability.* Paris: UNESCO.

Four slogans for cultural change: an evolving place-based, imaginative and ecological learning experience

Sean Blenkinsop
Simon Fraser University, Canada

This article focuses primarily on our research group's year of preparation before the opening of a new K-7 publicly funded ecological 'school' for students aged 5–12. The article begins with a discussion of the reasons for seeking ways to change the values of a culture which fails to confront the consequences of its destructive practices, and for looking for a new approach to ecological education which sees the more-than-human world as an integral part of the learning situation. Five principles are introduced and explained—principles that have grown out of the evolving experience of the research group, and then four 'slogans', which have served to guide the ongoing work of development, are described and illustrated. As part of the purpose of this project to change social and cultural values, the change of values within the research group during its ongoing work is also explored.

Introduction

Rachel Carson's *Silent spring* (1962) is the historical watershed for environmental awareness. Educators soon became interested in environmental concerns, and today environmental education is approaching its half century, but we would be hard-pressed to point to significant gains. Populations are still increasing, degradation of the planet continues, resource consumption is growing exponentially, and those who are most responsible—the financially privileged of the West and North-fail to confront the problems and even deny them. Ironically, they are also those most likely to have been exposed to environmental education. There have certainly been gains; the environment continues to be a concern for many, the 3 Rs of reduce, reuse and recycle are still current, and individuals and communities are making decisions and concessions to protect the environment and change behaviour. All of these may be attributed to the work, energy and care of environmental educators and activists, and one can only assume that things would have been much worse were it not for their efforts. Yet it appears to have been extremely hard to change behaviour in a significant way. Why? To answer this question this article will first review three different styles of environmental education that have been practised over the years and, in so doing, make clear why it is that the project described throughout the rest of the article has made the particular decisions it has.

The first style of environmental education, drawing on those Platonic roots which suggest that knowing the good equates to doing the good, focuses on having students understand the problem, thus enabling them to make informed decisions; if students understand the environment, its challenges and relationship to humans, then they will act in ways commensurate with its ongoing well-being. The range of curricula adopting this educational approach includes everything from environmental science programmes which introduce students to concepts such as life, systems, or interdependence, to classroom discussions, designed to shock and induce awe, in which students encounter the litany of problems faced by the globe and, it is hoped, find ways to respond to and resolve them.

A second style of environmental education, drawing on more recent work in eco-psychology (Roszak, Gomes & Kanner, 1995) and autobiography (Cobb, 2004; Tomashow, 1996) allows students to spend time in natural settings in order to build relationships with the more-than-human world. Such experience might take the form of wilderness trips, silent retreats, or growing gardens and caring for animals. The idea behind this second approach is that without relationships it is unlikely students will develop an interest in the natural world, and most unlikely that they will change their behaviour.

A third, more recent approach is theoretical rather than practical. This is in part because it is a response to the limited success of the first two, but also because it is more difficult to implement. This approach has tended to focus on the boundaries imposed by culture, the problem inherent in the worldview of the North and West. It is argued that the environmental challenges of today are a product of modernity and, if there is to be change, then it needs to happen at the cultural level. The eco-feminists (Merchant, 1980; Plumwood, 2002), for example, situate the problem in patriarchy and its constant marginalisation and oppression of the non-male and non-human. Lynn White (1967) suggested that Christianity is responsible, while, according to Bowers (1997), the problem lies in the very root metaphors upon which Western culture is built. Whatever the reason, each theory leads to the conclusion that there needs to be seismic cultural change, from a worldview which is non-environmental in its practices and its structural underpinnings (e.g. axiology, ontology, cosmology, etc.), to one that is ecologically grounded. It is in response to the need for a cultural change—which is also a moral change—that our project was undertaken; we want to know if it is possible to change fundamental values—in this case ecological values—of our society and culture by means of a radically different educational approach.

An educational project for cultural change: towards a place-based, imaginative, ecological 'school'

In February 2010 the Community University Research Alliance (special Environmental Call), a branch of the Social Sciences and Humanities Research Council of

Canada, agreed to fund our research project[1]: 'Aligning Education and Sustainability in Maple Ridge, BC: A Study of Place-Based Ecological Schooling'. In November the board of trustees of school district 42 voted unanimously to go ahead with the project. The 'school' opened in September 2011 with three 'classes'[2] and a total of 60 students, ages 5–12. In order to provide a context for the later discussion here are two passages from our original submission.[3]

From the Summary of Proposed Research:

> Public education systems, across the industrialized world, tend to be isolated from local processes of knowledge-building, planning, and decision-making for sustainability. In addition, although efforts have been made over the last three decades to include environmental education in school programs, their overall impact has been limited. Environmental education programs are rarely integrated with the mainstream curriculum, are typically of short duration, often lack theoretical or methodological sophistication, and show little compelling evidence of having long-term effects on most students' thinking about or engagement with diverse others including the natural world. (Blenkinsop & Fettes, 2009, p. 3)

And further, from the Statement of Relevance:

> One potentially fruitful approach to developing a deeper understanding of this problem, and of what might be needed to resolve it, is therefore to study the development of a public school expressly aligned with local environmental management and planning for sustainability. Such research, as outlined in this proposal, will be long-term and collaborative, and address not only issues of curriculum and pedagogy, but also school administration, school-community relationships, teacher development, learning outcomes and social impact. (Blenkinsop & Fettes, 2009, p. 5)

This article is the first publication to emerge from the project and focuses on some of the challenges, discussions and decisions that have arisen thus far. I[4] shall first present a number of principles that we developed to serve both as a guide and a corrective to future work. Although it is traditional to establish principles at the outset, as in this article, because of the nature of this project, which fundamentally challenges traditional values, the principles were developed as the members of the research group themselves developed. There were no fixed objectives at the start, deliberately not; principles emerged slowly and with difficulty out of the collective learning of the group, and as the understanding of an ecological worldview and a commitment to that view established itself.

Principles and values[5]

We seek to grow relationships and nurture practices of learning and teaching that embody the following principles and values.

1. Place and community. We cultivate learning in, about, with and from local places. This includes spending extensive time immersed in the outdoors, dialoguing with the diverse people connected to these places, and exploring the meaning of places in the context of the broader community associated with them, its past and future. Our hope is to nurture and develop an inclusive educational community deeply rooted in place.

This pairing of place and community may seem redundant. However, one of our specific aims has been to respond directly to what Val Plumwood (2002) has called the 'backgrounding' of the non-human world; it simply drops out of sight and out of mind. We are trying to find ways to have the non-human world constantly present by holding meetings outdoors, and by constant reference to it in our discussions. We also propose that it might play an active role in our students' learning. If the natural world is one of the active co-teachers in our school (Blenkinsop & Beeman, 2010), then we learn not only in and about place, but also from it. We believe that we do not just learn from nature in the way Emerson (1968) suggested, but that nature has an active role in the process of our learning.

This sense of the other-than-human world as being active, co-creative and even speaking to us is an important theme that appears several times in this article and deserves a short discussion to help elucidate some of the ways we are conceptualising the layers of active engagement on the part of nature.

The most easily understood layer is that of direct encounter and interpretation. This layer of communication is offered to us continually: a house finch sings heartily from a tree top, a large V of honking geese passes overhead flying south, a maple's leaves are turning red and gold, Orion's belt has just appeared in the sky—all of them clear signs carrying readily interpreted messages.

However, the natural world can engage us at a deeper and more complex level. Baird Callicott (1989) tells of how Aldo Leopold[6] would place his graduate students in an area where each had to document its current state and its history, flora, fauna, soils, human influences—a complete picture of the place, one which might be used to predict its future. At this layer the conversation is extensive and involves careful listening, yet the interpretation still remains solely in the hands of the human, although quotes such these from Leopold might suggest differently.

> Every farm woodland, in addition to yielding lumber, fuel, and posts, should provide its owner a liberal education. This crop of wisdom never fails, but it is not always harvested. (Leopold, 1989, p. 73)

> Every farm is a textbook on animal ecology; woodsmanship is the translation of the book. (Leopold, 1989, p. 81)

The final layer involves a shift in the human encounter with the natural world: the world literally speaks to us, not in our language but in its own; we become, as it were, bilingual. No longer separated from the more-than-human world, we have become a part of it; an ontological shift has occurred. Two brief examples might help. The first comes from Gregory Bateson's (2000) description of the man finding his way in a pitch-black cave by using a cane. Bateson's point is that it is hard to tell where I, the man, begin and where the cane ends. The same point is made by an exercise I do with pairs of students. One of the pair closes his or her eyes, while the other brings an object close enough for one finger to touch it. The goal is to identify the object, but the blindfolded partner must describe everything the finger is experiencing; s/he must say for each piece of information, 'the finger is telling me that the object is …'. Students experience both a sense of their own boundaries, but also how, if these boundaries move, who speaks, who is being spoken to, and where self might lie can manifestly change.

The second example comes from some work with Aboriginal Elders in Northern Ontario, Michael Paul (an Elder) says:

> you wake up
> and you have no game plan
> and you just go out
>
> maybe you want to paddle
> down the lake today
>
> or go up the river
> go down the river
>
> but no matter how you feel
> it's you
>
> this land is telling you
> what to do

> [Author 1 writes:] I understand Michael Paul to perceive himself, his surroundings, the place he calls home, to be part of a very complex identity that is composed of, as far as I know, at least two aspects of the same thing, which to me would usually appear to be distinct. These are what we would conventionally see as the human body as it is delineated from the world outside it through the large organ of the skin, and the world that is sometimes immediately and sometimes more distantly responsible for that body's survival. (Beeman & Blenkinsop, 2008, p. 2)

These, then, are three ways by which nature might actively engage with us as co-teacher and interlocutor. Our hope is that the students at the 'school' will develop the ability to communicate with and learn from nature in all these ways.

2. Nature, ecology and sustainability.[7] We cultivate learning in natural settings, where we listen for what the more-than-human world has to teach us. Through the cycle of the seasons and the years, knowledge of ecosystems will be built gradually so that diversity, complexity and sustainability become part of our understanding of the world. How to live sustainably in this place is an ongoing question in everything we do.

Part of the goal is to continually make the natural world a presence and a partner in the project. The choice of 'ecology' rather than the more recognisable 'environment' was made for several reasons, but primarily to side-step some of the metaphorical baggage. 'Environment' has tended to be understood as an entity set apart from humanity and, when coupled with education, evokes one or other of the first two trends in environmental education discussed above, but rarely the third, i.e. the more radical integration of the human and more-than-human worlds.

Thus, the hope was to pre-empt that difficulty. The word ecology also reminds us that within the project we understand ecosystems to be exemplars of sustainable communities. They are places that have much to teach us as we move towards a more ecological worldview. Sustainability is troublesome as a concept because it is often used in connection with technical, and even environmentally destructive, projects. 'Sustainable development' has been used to describe everything from fish farming to the Alberta tar sands. Its recognisability is, however, useful and the task is to link it to nature and ecology.

3. Inquiry and possibility. We cultivate a spirit of inquiry involving everyone: the natural world,[8] students, parents, community members, teachers and researchers alike. We are committed to exploring multiple pathways of learning and teaching that engage many different ways of knowing and forms of knowledge. Meaningful, authentic, locally inspired individual, group and community projects play an important part in this process.

The choice of the word 'possibility' was made because of its reference to existential philosophy. For the existentialists the notion of possibility invokes the seemingly endless number of choices available to each of us, to our familial groupings, to our communities. Through the act of choosing we are, in Sartre's (1946) words, both creating value and creating the kind of world we want to live in. We need to allow each other and ourselves to make those choices, live with the possibilities and the accompanying responsibilities, and accept the challenge of change rather than passively adapting to an imperfect world.

4. Interdependence and flourishing. We cultivate an appreciation of people both as unique individuals and as members of nested families, communities and places. We seek to understand the complex ways in which we can help each other flourish, and how to build relationships and systems that contribute to such flourishing. We aim to foster respect, care and health in everything we do.

By linking interdependence and flourishing we remind ourselves of the work of philosopher and ecologist Arne Naess (2005) who suggested that one of the pivotal roles and moral responsibilities of humans was to support the maximisation of diversity, complexity and flourishing for all, human and more-than-human alike. The purpose of this principle is to remind us of the danger of trying to sustain, through our failure to choose, a way of living that is currently inequitable and destructive to many while, simultaneously, we need to remember that collectively we should help one another to reach her, his, or its potential. This conjunction of interdependence and flourishing has also led us into an interesting discussion around assessment. If interdependence is a basic principle, how do we evaluate the learning of students, and how do we assess contribution to the community?

5. Imagination and integration. We cultivate imagination in teaching and learning as a key to deeper understanding, creativity and responsiveness to place and community. We look for ways to integrate learning across the curriculum, bridging language arts, sciences, histories, geographies, mathematics, physical and social skills. We develop educational practices and materials that nurture a sense of wholeness in learning and teaching.

Possibility depends upon the imagination and, contrary to popular opinion, the imagination is not unlimited. We think that by cultivating imagination, facing a world in all its complexity and expanding the range of our experience we shall be better able to affect cultural change.

Kieran Egan's (1997) work on imaginative education will serve as a guide and help us move away from education as it is currently practised and towards a more ecological vision. Egan's work, though not ecological, is an example of a philosophy of education that has stepped outside the normal paradigm. Building on some of Vygotsky's work, Egan suggests that there are five ways of understanding—somatic, mythic, romantic, philosophic, ironic—which recapitulate our culture's linguistic evolution. Each way comes with a cognitive tool kit, provided by the culture and assumed by the individual through the imagination, helping the individual to make sense of the world.[9]

Using this work as a starting point we are beginning to postulate that the more-than-human world, and not just our particular cultures, might also offer tools for understanding that can be engaged and developed through careful teaching. Gillian Judson (2010) has undertaken some interesting work in this regard with her 'place-making' tool.

The principles were not our starting point. Rather it was the following four 'slogans' which served as a preliminary guide to our group as the project evolved. Each slogan has gained credibility within the research group and, by explaining them in turn, together with specific examples, we hope that the project will become clearer.

Slogan #1: 'Everything is up for grabs'

This first slogan rests upon our assumption that the argument for cultural change is convincing: that the idea of school, at least in a modern Western context, is embedded in an ecologically and socially unjust and dysfunctional worldview (cf. Bowers, 1997; Merchant, 1980; Orr, 1992; Plumwood, 2002). Thus the attempt to effect change calls for more than superficial adjustments of current practice, it requires a new approach based on radically different values. A further implication is that everything within a particular cultural milieu has been shaped and coloured by it. This does not imply that everything must necessarily be discarded, but rather that everything deserves scrutiny and reappraisal. To further complicate the challenge posed by this slogan, education is usually not the driving force of a worldview; rather it is a product of that worldview, and its goal is to socialise the next generation into the mainstream culture. As a result, early education tends to over-emphasise the prevailing culture, presenting it as a kind of caricature. Thus, we, and those cited above, believe that today's schools project an environmentally and socially unjust worldview, the major features of which are values, such as order, hierarchy, competition, compliance, standardisation, seen as all-important, as, too, are notions of what knowledge is and where learning occurs, individualisation, what is good and bad. Separation of human beings from the natural world is just one of the underlying concepts.

The task we set ourselves in the project group was to open everything that occurs in and around schools to question, examination and, if necessary and possible, change. This includes such aspects of school life as bells, schedules, age-groupings, class make-up, files, the registration process (we held our registration outdoors, under a bandstand in the city's central park, and at the beginning of February), and also deeper, more complex questions of content, pedagogy, assessment, student development, learning, governance, and place; we have gained the support of the district not to have school buildings at all. Finally, there are the central philosophical questions of epistemology, ontology, axiology, cosmology, discussion of which has allowed us to begin to conceptualise the role of traditions and creation stories in sustaining a culture. Last of all there is metaphor.

Rather than attempting to explore each item on this list, I will focus on metaphor, since it has been so central to our discussions on this project. As we all do, our students live immersed in a plethora of social and cultural messages. The structure and function of schools tells us what is important and what is not, what to be aware of and what to ignore, how systems work, and how the culture works. Elsewhere we have written more specifically about the semiotics of education (Creeping Snowberry,[10] 2010), but for the present the point is that these messages reflect the culture. Within schools, environmental education may be undone by the conflicting messages created by these cultural artefacts. For example, a teacher may spend the day discussing interdependence, then a bell sounds summoning students to a different classroom and a different discipline, or homework is returned with each student receiving an individual, independent mark. Such mixed metaphors are all too common, and a major challenge has been to try to find metaphors appropriate to an ecologically based education. What are we saying to the community when we use metaphors? What are their effects—positive or negative—and how does one underpin or undermine the effect of metaphors? This last question becomes especially challenging if the metaphors are what Bowers (1997) refers to as 'root metaphors', metaphors such as progress, individualism or mechanism, which act as the support structure for the culture.

An example which arose at the outset of the project is the word 'school'.[11] What images come to mind, when we hear the word 'school'? If you are like most North Americans, you have images of rectangular buildings, with a playing field, a parking lot, some fences, some play structures perhaps, and maybe somewhere a tree or two. But now go deeper! What else appears? Classrooms, industrial tiling, a place where learning happens, the way to get ahead, pain and boredom, bells, compliance with imposed regulation, distinct classes, line-ups, objective-driven curricula. We begin to see how this metaphor of 'school' carries with it the epistemology, ontology and axiology of the culture, how lurking in every locker, from the number and lock on the front to the textbooks and gym shoes inside, are confirmations of a particular worldview. Our group had to ask itself what had to happen if these metaphors arising from the word 'school' were in conflict with the underlying goals and values of our projected ecological learning experience.

The obvious answer was to change metaphors, but the new metaphors had to let the wider community—school officials, teachers, prospective parents—begin to involve itself in our learning project, to understand that things would be different, but not shake prevailing notions so much that it became alarmed or even hostile. Thus, we are searching for new metaphors that are able to strike that delicate balance between 'dissonnating'[12] and supporting, so that each person can find his or her way to hear and incorporate this new way of looking. The result of this metaphorical challenge is that the project leaders as a group are continually thinking not only about what we do, but also about how we do it. For example, we hold many meetings outdoors or in non-school buildings in order to break out of old metaphors and create, then support new ones as they appear and are applicable. Even the language we use is affected, as we try to be aware of the implications of our words: administrator, environment, governance. It has been fascinating to hear members of the school district, the municipality and partner groups use the expression 'hearth keepers' to describe the board of directors, and to observe how this language has led them to begin to take on roles as protectors and nurturers of a new vision. The superintendent of schools now agrees that the school can not be housed in a regular building, since this would immediately send the wrong message. Yet we need to be constantly vigilant, for almost any metaphorical inconsistency[13] could derail the project. Everything is up for grabs!

Slogan #2: Maintain 'hyperactive pessimism'

This slogan comes from Michel Foucault's (1984) description of himself as an ongoing and suspicious cultural questioner and also his underlying sense that change is not so easily achieved as it might appear. We have noted our need to be constantly vigilant, indeed, to be hyperactive in that vigilance; but why pessimistic?

Let us start with an image. Think for a moment of a tree. What came into your mind; trunk, branches, greenery? Most often it is the sense of sight that is used when we conjure up an image, and, if Annie Dillard (1988) is to be believed, this image is based on what we think we see, our cultural narrative of tree, rather than that which we actually see. Not only do we not make use of our other senses, but we also ignore aspects of the tree, such as the root systems in the earth drawing in nutrients. Now let us take that tree, roots and all, as a metaphor for a worldview. If the purpose of our 'school' project is cultural change, then every aspect of it must be explored, examined and approved, or rejected, right down to the very last rhizome. And, bearing in mind Foucault's pessimism, we start from his position of total suspicion. Modern Western culture has deep roots that reach into our minds and souls, our thoughts and beliefs. Anything that is easy to us or is self-evident, is probably so because it stems from our cultural formation.[14] Thus the slogan reminds us to assume the stance of pessimism, to be forever suspicious and be hyperactive in our vigilance.

To carry our metaphor of the tree a little further, we know that trees age, die and are replaced very slowly. In our project we are not ridding ourselves of everything; trees do not do this.[15] We are examining every piece that we include, whether new or old. It was to help us in this endeavour that we began to develop the principles that are listed and discussed above.

Slogan #3: 'This is gonna hurt'

Pain has already been experienced in our research group; one member has said that if she had known how much work and pain were involved, she would not have joined us.[16] If we are going to engage in cultural and personal change, there is going to be pain, which manifests itself in a variety of ways and can be different for each person. Cultural change is a project of transformation and, although this experience can be wonderful and freeing, it is not easy. It may in fact be the litmus test for transformation, and the reason why philosophers such as Kierkegaard (1954) and Sartre (1964) have described change in terms of anxiety and even nausea.

Pain occurs at moments of fundamental change because, as we apprehend a new awareness, former deeply held beliefs and behaviour are thrown into question. The ground upon which we have built our lives appears to be less stable and in conflict with this new consciousness. Things we have done in the past are no longer acceptable to us, but not only are our personal histories becoming troublesome, so too is the ecological record of our culture. Those of us involved in this project might well remember occasions on which we have deliberately harmed the environment, times when we have chosen to not know what we were doing, or when we have profited from the destructive behaviour of our forebears and our culture. There will be pain, too, because of our relationships, personal and professional, and any change that I experience has implications for my family, my community and my work situation. How do you continue to teach in an educational system, in which you were formerly comfortable, when you become aware of the ecological damage it is doing? What if priorities you have shared with others (parents, partners, friends, children) for your entire life change, and those others now encounter a substantially new person, a different you? Such questions and their resultant levels of pain are becoming apparent within the research group.

One particular manifestation of pain, particularly amongst those who have been involved in our research group the longest, I shall call ecological double consciousness. It appears to be similar to the alienation described by W.E.B. Dubois (1968) when discussing the black experience. One of the earliest conversations we had in the group was about the need for a role we euphemistically called 'the translator'. We felt that the project would need someone who could interpret the values and practices of our 'school' for those whose entire experience had been in the traditional education system. If, for example, our 'school' was to use mastery, flourishing and interdependence as its means of assessment, then someone would have to translate those results into something the school district and the larger community understood. It soon became apparent that this was not simply a job of translating, but also one of protecting. The translator would also act as a buffer for us, thereby allowing the teachers and learners a safe space to develop within their new environment without constant intervention from outside. It was at this point that some of the first symptoms of this ecological double consciousness began to appear. For Dubois, the double consciousness was the experience of being a black man in the USA. He describes having two consciousnesses, one that adopts the white racist position of the standard culture, and another that tries to take pride and a sense of worth in his own black soul, as he calls it. Thus, not only is there a dominant culture that denigrates and marginalises the black man, but there is also a part of the person himself who accepts that position. The result is a division between the two selves and between oneself and the world, a barrier through which it is hard to pass.

What became apparent for several members of the group was that they were experiencing a similar sort of internal and external division. As we talked and began to elaborate our ideas and values, they began to discover a new self, one which was familiar, as though they were coming home or coming out of the closet and into their own authenticity as 'ecological people'. But another self was also appearing, a self that was dealing with the outside world—whether partners, parents or the school district—one who had to be vigilant, not too trusting, aware of not being listened to, and, with regard to the project, of being mocked and even threatened. A gap was appearing between the translators and the outside world, and the gap seemed to be between one's authentic self and that person who needed to be accepted and understood outside our small group. People experienced turmoil as these two sides wrestled within them, and they wondered if the pain and suffering was worth it.

Since first encountering this problem, I have talked with many committed ecologists who admit to a similar experience, and it is not unlike that of gay and lesbian people, or of that described by Dubois. Although ecologists have not experienced the same level of personal violence, violence has certainly been directed at the more-than-human world.

This difficult experience—that for a time affected the personality of one member of our group—has had to be confronted. First, we have worked hard to establish a safe community within the research group and to build relationships of mutual trust. We have also insisted that people—especially the translators—spend time away from work. For most of us it has been interesting to discover that being in the natural world is where we feel the most safe, alive and well—a characteristic of the eco-person perhaps, but one we feel is important to honour for all of us.[17]

One final, encouraging note is that we have also been fortunate to build, over our three years of working together, good relationships with several of the senior administrators in the district, and their commitment to this ecological vision of education has meant that they, too, have become protectors and translators.

Slogan #4: 'When in doubt (which is likely much of the time given the previous slogans), remember the ecosystem'

This final slogan is one that appears to be currently gaining in importance within the project. It acts as a constant reminder of our commitment to the natural world and to thinking of it as an active partner in the entire project. It also acknowledges that, since the goal is a flourishing, diverse, complex and interdependent community, the best examples we have are ecosystems. When in doubt our first recourse is to ask what happens in an ecosystem. The issue could be governance, pedagogy, assessment and evaluation, or values. Whatever it might be, we turn to the ecosystem.

Assessment is, perhaps, the major challenge for anyone trying to effect educational change. How an educational system evaluates its students, and teachers for that matter, is an excellent indicator of a society's values and ideology. The current system tends to rely on individualised evaluation, hierarchical marking schemes and competition supported by epistemic interpretations which view knowledge as something which can be located, compartmentalised, accumulated and transferred. Where knowledge is contextual, emergent, relational and interactive,[18] and where the system rests, as appears to be the case in well-functioning natural systems, upon notions of interdependence, complexity, diversity, equity and a form of dynamic equilibrium, it is essential to ask what sort of evaluation is appropriate. The immediate answer is that we are not yet sure. However, here is a possible scenario.

It is the end of term, and the community has gathered to celebrate. Each class-grouping has put together a public display of their semester's work, and now pairs of students are meeting with teachers, care-givers, several chosen elders and/or community members, along with representatives of the natural world presented in imaginative ways.[19] This last, of course, might lead to the charge of anthropomorphism and a concern as to how nature is being interpreted or misrepresented, but we suggest, along the lines taken by Val Plumwood (2002), that this critique depends very much on the purpose of the anthropomorphism. The purpose of these groups of people concerned in the students' development is to explore learning through dialogue, a process both demonstrative and reflective that finds ways to support learning as a shared endeavour and also showcases the diversity of knowledge created, or not, in the case of any particular student within the larger community. Possible areas of exploration might include: skills[20] and strengths developed over the previous term and ways in which growth is demonstrated in the students themselves and in service to others, including the more-than-human world; examples of the complexities that have appeared; potential challenges that will need particular attention; areas of interest to explore in the coming term, together with suggestions of who or what might be able to contribute. Thus, the evaluation process becomes one of collective responsibility and commitment, of sharing in the learning programme, of exchanging ideas and experience, and of honouring achievement, while simultaneously setting projects for further learning.[21]

With regard to this slogan one of the challenges, enjoining us to remember the ecosystem, is that of interpretation. The history of science shows us how variable our understanding of the natural world has been over time. Interpretation often tells us more about the interpreter than about what is interpreted, and this is likely to be the case for us as well. Yet, at the very least this recourse to nature provides an invaluable moment of reflection and opens us to other possibilities. The group has also begun to form shared understandings of ecosystems, so that we are developing a common interpretation that has implications for decisions well beyond the bounds of the school.

Conclusion

We have undertaken the task and responsibility of changing values. We believe that the current values held and practices displayed by societies in the North and West with relation to the more-than-human world are wrong and destructive and that they need to be replaced by new values based on the conviction that ecosystems offer a model that has achieved some of the long-term richness and diversity of life, robustness of sustainability, and success of the membership that we require for our survival, and that the more-than-human world must become our teacher and interlocutor.

The principles and slogans that we have evolved and amended, and continue to amend, serve as our guides as we move into the first year of operation. They will also serve as the basis for the evaluation of our success, when we come to review our first year. No doubt further amendments will be needed.

At this point, as we review the process of preparation undergone in the development of the project, an interesting and unexpected outcome has been the effect this intense, collective work has had upon the moral development of those of us in the research group. As the principles and slogans gather significance and meaning they become important touchstones for us even beyond the limits of the project. They serve as a guide to decisions, as measures for questioning, and as criteria with which to examine decisions. For example, are we, as the research group, involved in a large community partnership, allowing new possibilities to arise spontaneously, or are we unilaterally and blindly making things happen the way we think they should? And how do we balance the spontaneous with the particular direction implied by a limited range of sought outcomes?

The principles and slogans are also being used as ways to alert us to problems inherent in what we are doing and in any direction we are proposing. Recently at a retreat it was brought to our attention, tearfully, that there is a sense within the larger group that some of us were doing too much and were in danger of harming not only ourselves but also the group. This concern arose from a deep care for the individuals in question and also for the integrity of the project, which was in danger of 'violating' its own principles. As a result we recognised that something had to change, but we also realised that our new values were being put to actual, living use. We did not set out to educate each other morally, but we found that we were changing morally as a result of this shared story that is the project.

Jean-Paul Sartre was once asked why he never wrote an ethics for existentialism. His response (1992) was that he felt ethics was the last part of a new paradigm to be developed, and that it needed to rise out of the tools, or ways of being, of the new paradigm. He also suggested that to begin to develop an ethics too early was to invoke the tools of the previous paradigm, thereby effectively distorting the new. My sense is that, in the case of this project, our moral education is emerging and evolving, as we live through the challenges we encounter each day. It develops as we build systems, ways of interacting, following, however tentatively, the direction indicated by our slogans and principles, and working to live, teach, and learn in more ecological, place-based and imaginative ways.

Acknowledgements

I would like to thank the editors and Paddy Blenkinsop for their comments, care and assistance in bringing this article to fruition. This research is generously supported by the Community and University Research Alliance Fund administered by the Social Sciences and Humanities Research Council of Canada.

Notes

1. For a more complete sense of this project and the large group of partners please see our website at http://schools.sd42.ca/es/
2. The quotation marks around 'school' and 'class' will be discussed later.
3. Readers may notice similarities to the writings and practices of others in these descriptions. We have drawn from many and some are referenced in the larger proposal. It is impossible to do justice to all the influences in this space.
4. The very notion of single authorship—including my authorship of this article—has been a part of ongoing discussions. As of yet, we have not reached a comfortable answer.
5. One interesting challenge that we have come up against in this process is a move by others to completely dismiss the project, its ideas and insights, by accusing it of utopianism. This is not, in fact, an unusual move in larger North American political discussions. Our sense is not of these principles and values as being fixed, or even achievable, but that they are, as it were, current signposts worth striving towards. We choose to imbue them with significance as we live into and towards them while remaining vigilant as to both their continued usefulness and their potential to reify into dogma.
6. A famous early environmental American writer and advocate.
7. Sustainability is a hugely charged political and philosophical term in today's world and one, among many, that we problematise on an ongoing basis. It has also become a site of overlap between the stated values and the curricular actuality of the school. For example, one important curricular activity at the school is fort-building. Yet the first site for the forts was rapidly denuded of all vegetation. It was either trampled or used as building material. This destruction led to some really interesting discussions with regard to rights, future well being, stewardship, ownership and governance (there was even a 'presidency' [interesting move for Canadian children] with bodyguards established at one point, along with the creation of a fairly sophisticated monetary system based on resources and knot-tying skills).
8. We are actively interested in this idea of nature as researcher.
9. For further information on Egan's work see any of his books, such as 1986, 1997, 2005.
10. Creeping Snowberry is an experiment in collective writing that involves many members of the research group.

11. One member of the research group has taken to using her fingers to physically place in parenthesis the word 'school' every time she refers to the project. Recently a community member commented 'How long are you going to keep doing that?', suggesting that this person understood that this school is different and was tired of being reminded.
12. This idea of teacher as dissonnator is drawn from the work of David Denton (1972) in *Existential reflections on teaching.*
13. In the case of the school building the danger lies in the metaphors that accompany that structure and the way that structure is understood within the current culture. In other situations, like moving from Parent Action Committee to Hearthkeepers, we have been seeking to support the metaphor of community. In referring to the natural world as teacher we both foreground/make it present and we also provide it with an active position rather than the more common passive version.
14. For example, a common response, upon first hearing of the project, is for a teacher to suggest that s/he is already doing what we are talking about. Although I do not doubt teachers are doing some things that align, our experience suggests that the changes they make are more likely to tinker than to be seismic. This is not in any way to place blame; we fully understand the realities of today's public school teacher. The point is that these changes are unlikely to be easy.
15. For example, trees will use previous tree roots and structures (channels, nitrogen-fixers, etc.) when they are in line with the new tree's purposes.
16. Interestingly, she also notes that now that she knows what she knows as a result of the project she can never go back to happily not knowing.
17. This was prior knowledge for some in the group but was a discovery for others.
18. This is at the edge of a much larger epistemological discussion, but it has become apparent that assuming knowledge is completely fragmentable and then gatherable in bricklike fashion and, as such, testable in a standardised multiple choice way is an incomplete reckoning of how and what we know.
19. The Bioregionalist's idea of a Council for all Beings (see: http://www.rainforestinfo.org.au/deep-eco/Joanna%20Macy.htm [accessed 19 April 2012]) may offer one possibility here as someone in the meeting takes on the role of a selected character of the natural world.
20. Language/metaphors seem to fail us regularly, in particular in this discussion. There are skills being learned by individuals but that metaphor, of skill, tends to isolate and simplify. The challenge for us is to find ways to question growth while mitigating potential hierarchies. The reality of this discussion is that we continue to fumble.
21. It has become apparent to the entire project that the question of 'evaluation' and 'assessment' is the elephant in the room for the project, and for education as a whole. The struggle with report cards and with finding more complex and nuanced ways of thinking about and demonstrating knowledge is very difficult at many levels. One noticeable success has been a kind of storytelling with the support of creative objects, that the students put on for their parents. There were moments of understanding that shone through for everyone. However, this is just a start and we are a long way from finding a range of ecologically sensitive and pedagogically appropriate ways to recognise, demonstrate and honour learning that is complex, diverse and shared.

References

Bateson, G. (2000). *Steps to an ecology of mind.* Chicago, IL: University of Chicago Press.

Beeman, C., & Blenkinsop S. (2008). Dwelling-telling diversity: initial key to an ecological worldview. Proceedings of the 28th Annual Philosophy of Education Society of Australasia Conference, December, 2007. Available on double CD set, see http://www.pesa.org.au/04cal.htm (accessed 10 November 2010).

Blenkinsop, S., & Beeman, C. (2010). The world as co-teacher: Learning to work with a peerless colleague. *Trumpeter, 26*(3), 26–39.

Blenkinsop, S., & Fettes, M. (2009). Aligning education and sustainability in Maple Ridge, BC: A study of place-based ecological schooling. Successful Social Sciences and Humanities Research Council, Environmental Community University Research Alliance Grant Application.

Bowers, C.A. (1997). *The culture of denial: Why the environmental movement needs a strategy for reforming universities and public schools*. Albany, NY: State University of New York Press.

Callicott, J.B. (1989). *In defense of the Land Ethic: Essays in environmental philosophy*. Albany, NY: State University of New York Press.

Carson, R. (1962). *Silent spring*. Greenwich: Fawcett.

Cobb, E. (2004). *The ecology of imagination in childhood*. Putnam, CT: Spring Publishing.

Creeping Snowberry (2010). 'Why are those leaves red?': Making sense of the complex symbols: ecosemiotics in education. *Trumpeter, 26*(3), 50–60.

Denton, D. (1972). *Existential reflections on teaching*. North Quincy, MA: The Christopher Publishing House.

Dillard, A. (1988). *Pilgrim at Tinker Creek*. New York, NY: Harper Perennial.

Dubois, W.E.B. (1968). *The soul of black folks: Essays and sketches*. New York, NY: Johnson Reprint.

Egan, K. (1986). *Teaching as storytelling*. London: Althouse Press.

Egan, K. (1997). *The educated mind: How cognitive tools shape our understanding*. Chicago, IL: University of Chicago Press.

Egan, K. (2005). *An imaginative approach to teaching*. San Francisco, CA: Jossey-Bass.

Emerson, R.W. (1968). *The complete works*. Boston, MA: Houghton-Mifflin.

Foucault, M. (1984). *The Foucault reader*. New York, NY: Vintage.

Judson, G. (2010). *A new approach to ecological education: Engaging students' imaginations in their world*. New York, NY: Peter Lang.

Kierkegaard, S. (1954). *Fear and trembling, and the sickness unto death*, trans. W. Lowrie. Garden City, NY: Doubleday.

Leopold, A. (1989). *A Sand County almanac*. New York, NY: Oxford University Press.

Merchant, C. (1980). *The death of nature: Women, ecology and the scientific revolution*. New York, NY: Harper Collins.

Naess, A. (2005). The basics of deep ecology. *Trumpeter, 21*(1), 61–71.

Orr, D.W. (1992). *Ecological literacy: Education and the transition to a postmodern world*. Albany, NY: State University of New York Press.

Plumwood, V. (2002). *Environmental culture*. New York, NY: Routledge.

Roszak, T., Gomes, M., & Kanner, A. (Eds.). (1995). *Ecopsychology: Restoring the earth, healing the mind*. San Francisco, CA: Sierra Club.

Sartre, J.P. (1946). Existentialism is a humanism. In W. Kaufmann (Ed.), *Existentialism from Dostoyevsky to Sartre*. New York, NY: Meridian Publishing Company.

Sartre, J.P. (1964). *Nausea*, trans. L. Alexander. New York, NY: New Directions Publishing Company.

Sartre, J.P. (1992). *Notebooks for an ethics*. Chicago, IL: University of Chicago Press.

Thomashow, M. (1996). *Ecological identity: Becoming a reflective environmentalist*. Cambridge, MA: MIT Press.

White, L. (1967). The historical roots of our ecological crisis. *Science, 155*, 1203–1207.

Mountain guides: between ethics and socioeconomic trends

Thierry Long[a], Damien Bazin[b] and Bernard Massiéra[c]

[a]Laboratory of Cognitive and Social Psychology and Anthropology (LAPCOS), University of Nice Sophia-Antipolis, France; [b]Research Group in Law, Economics and Management (GREDEG) & Higher Institute of Economics and Management (ISEM), University of Nice Sophia-Antipolis, France; [c]Laboratory of Human Motricity, Education, Sport and Health (LAMHESS), University of Nice Sophia-Antipolis, France

This study analysed mountain guides' representations of environmental responsibility and explored the paradox that these professionals face: using nature as a source of income while trying to preserve it. The study was mainly guided by the philosophical literature on this topic and made use of the concepts of sustainable development and nature. This exploratory work therefore contributes to the new field of environmental social psychology. Semi-structured interviews were conducted and the qualitative analysis showed that mountain guides have a very sensitive and contemplative approach to moral aspects of our relationship with nature, which they try to transmit to their clients. They believe that this is a way to educate people about sustainable development, but this term emerged as quite vague for them, and they expressed the opinion that it might hide other concerns, such as to make translating it into moral conduct a difficult matter and to compromise their identity as moral actors.

Introduction

Sport is commonly viewed as the structure *par excellence* for promoting socialisation. According to sporting and political institutions, it provides a powerful means for teaching social skills, respect for others, the value of hard work, and so on (e.g. Olympic Charter,[1] p. 14). The ultimate goal of this socialisation process is to build respectful citizens who feel responsible for the future of their society (e.g. Sport for Development and Peace by the United Nations).[2] Yet, sport as a support to civic education has recently shown its limits (financial corruption, doping, violence inside and outside the playgrounds, etc.). Since science first dealt with this issue (Arnold, 1997; Bredemeier & Shields, 1986), sport as a humanist endeavour has shown evidence of weakening (Long, 2008). Instead sport seems to be increasingly dominated by functional reasoning, oriented toward high performance and social recognition (Long, Pantaléon, Bruant & d'Arripe-Longueville, 2006).

In spite of this, sport has been given a new ethical challenge: to transmit ecological awareness to its practitioners. Outdoor activities (mountain biking, rafting, trekking, sea sports such as surfing, etc.) have greatly developed in recent years and, according to Loret (1995), these sports exemplify postmodern values, such as individualism, freedom, hedonism and so on. Many of these activities have had a negative ecological impact, mainly because of the constant presence of sport practitioners in natural spaces (Mounet, 2007). We must therefore question the veracity and relevance of this new mission: to engage people in 'sustainable development'.

This study examined the sense of responsibility for the environment demonstrated by outdoor activities instructors in order to analyse their reasoning on this issue and its moral significance. We chose to focus on mountain guides as they stand on the frontline regarding the transmission of ecological awareness. However, these professionals face a paradox about how to manage the economic stakes (as they earn money from these activities) and the environmental stakes of their profession. How do they cope with this paradox? How do they combine economic, technical, hedonistic and ecological issues? The findings of this study will be analysed from the perspective of contemporary ideologies and discussed with regard to the principle of environmental responsibility developed by Jonas (1984).

1. Theoretical framework

1.1. The concept of sustainable development

The concept of 'sustainable development' emerged in the 1980s as a public-sector concern and not as an intellectual issue (Godard, 1994). The Brundtland report (United Nations World Commission on Environment and Development (UNWCED), 1987) and the 1992 United Nations conference on the environment and development in Rio de Janeiro (Agenda 21) popularised this notion. Yet Pezzey (1989) and Elliot (1999) pointed out that this concept has at least 70 definitions. The most usual definition was given by the Brundtland report (UNWCED, 1987, p. 51): 'development that meets the needs of the present without compromising the ability of future generations to meet their own needs.' When interpreted as a guide for conduct this definition becomes a moral imperative, and it seemed relevant to our study as it fits well with Jonas' 'imperative of responsibility', the environmental responsibility that is presented in section 1.2 of this article. However, vagueness and contradiction persist, as underlined by others (Bonnett, 2002; Elliot, 1999). First, what does 'development' mean?

According to Elliot (1999), 'development' is used in many fields, especially economics. For Ballet, Dubois and Mahieu (2004, p. 4), development by definition leads to structural changes in a complex socioeconomic reality. Development for these authors is thus mainly considered from an economic point of view, 'by definition'. Yet, 'by definition', development is also associated with notions of 'expansion' (in time or space), 'blooming' (biologically, morally, spiritually, etc.), 'progress' and 'growth', to name just a few (see *Encyclopædia Britannica*).[3]

Finally, environmental sustainability emphasises the battle against pollution, the preservation of non-renewable resources, energy saving and the transmission of natural capital to future generations (Ballet et al., 2004, p. 3). The means for meeting these objectives are varied (including the precautionary principle of 'protecting' non-renewable resources and 'clean' development; that is to say, vague concepts that prescribe no precise conduct; even the word 'clean' is written in quotation marks, a symbol of this imprecision).

From an ideological or philosophical point of view (Elliot, 1999), two extreme positions regarding the protection of nature can be highlighted: a 'technocentric' or anthropocentric ideology (Bonnett, 2002), which assumes that human needs come first and nature must be transformed—although with great care—in order to build a more comfortable world, as opposed to an 'ecocentric' ideology, which insists on respect for the central role of nature, in which humans are just an element.

Reflection about sustainable development arose from the growing awareness of the vulnerability of nature, and protecting nature has today become a human responsibility, as we will now show.

1.2. The concept of environmental responsibility

Responsibility is a multidimensional concept. In France, it was mainly developed during and after the Revolution of 1789, at a time in history when individuals could be held accountable to others for their acts or decisions and could take charge of their destinies beyond traditional determinism (Schlegel, 2000). In the nineteenth century, responsibility became a legal concept in civil and criminal law. The legal sense of responsibility remains focused on notions of transgression, guilt and sanction, which are simplistic categories that exclude a moral dimension (Etchegoyen, 1999). In the twentieth century, responsibility took on a political and humanist meaning. From this perspective, responsibility referred to those individuals who were conscientious and engaged in their communities, as well as to even the most spontaneous and informal initiatives to help others (Appel, 1993; Levinas, 1969).

The concept of environmental responsibility fits well with this humanist perspective. It was developed by the philosopher Hans Jonas (1984), who qualified it as the 'imperative of responsibility', and it is surely the main connotation for responsibility in the twenty-first century. Jonas is a philosopher of nature whose ultimate goal is the sustainability of humanity. He advocates individual responsibility for the perpetuation of life, especially now when we have the power to transform and destroy nature and thus ourselves. The industrialisation of our societies greatly diminished our awareness of the symbolic and physical power of nature over humans. Nature has become attackable and workable and thus perishable and vulnerable. These latter characteristics are exactly why nature is our moral responsibility, just as the vulnerability of another person brings out our sense of responsibility (Levinas, 1969): 'if humans act responsibly, it is because they possess power that is likely to turn against their own freedom' (Bazin, 2007, p. 7).[4] In this sense, the ethics under consideration does not directly concern nature but human life: protecting a tree is not an end in itself, but protecting human life through this tree has value and ontological sense. Jonas thus distinguishes his thinking from the ideology of deep ecology and totally subscribes to a humanist philosophy.

1.3. Sustainable development and outdoor activities

Based on the above reflections on sustainability, we can now focus on a field for applying this concept: outdoor activities. After describing the relationships between these activities and nature, we will discuss the main actors, that is, professional outdoor activities instructors.

1.3.1. Outdoor activities and nature. In line with the ecological awareness first expressed in the 1960s (Vignal & Chazaud, 2001), outdoor activities have steadily grown in popularity. Pociello (1981, 1995) described this phenomenon as 'the ecologisation' of sport. We think that this word is incorrect, as outdoor activities are not necessarily ecological activities; some simply are performed in a natural setting, which is very different. Vignal and Chazaud (2001) highlighted the contradiction in their findings between the 'ecologisation' of outdoor activities and people's beliefs in a still 'pure' nature, which refers to wilderness. They interpreted this paradox as an urban reasoning process, in which nature has become an object of consumption instead of an object of protection. Mounet, Nicollet and Rocheblave (2000) examined the environmental impact of outdoor activities and indicated a common path in the development of these activities. They first develop informally and quietly within a small community of sportsmen and sportswomen 'in the know' (and without specific facilities). Word spreads and, when a critical mass of practitioners is reached, the natural setting is appropriately equipped (and is thus no longer natural!). Nature then becomes a large 'playground'.

1.3.2. Outdoor activities instructors. Outdoor activities instructors work in a sector where the stakes are ill-defined. They deal with a vague concept—sustainable development—and they also deal with new professional activities in which nature functions as an economic sector. Mounet (2007) noted that outdoor activities practitioners know little about ecology (except mountain guides, whose knowledge of the environment is part of their service to clients). In their qualitative study on these professionals, Bouhaoula and Chifflet (2001) observed that their choice of profession was mainly determined by pleasure and a passion for nature. Yet very few concerns about the ecological and ethical stakes were noted. Corneloup and

Bourdeau (2002) added that these professionals were affected by 'managerial contamination', which was one of the reasons why they have lost a part of their original predisposition towards nature and the mountains. They often must conform to the current management standards of the companies for whom they may work. In another study, Bessy and Naria (2004) focused on the development of outdoor activities on Réunion Island, a French overseas department. According to these authors, 'sustainable development constantly forces us to question the social goals of our actions on the planet through the trio of economy, environment and society' (Bessy & Naria, 2004, p. 2). From an environmental perspective, these authors specified that, in spite of the potential degradation caused by some sports, outdoor activities also contribute to the protection of nature through various means: the organisation of specifically arranged areas for practice in order to avoid anarchism, the promotion of awareness of the symbiosis between humans and nature, and the initiation of individuals as potential protectors by professional instructors or activists (guides, Forest National Organisation, Surf Rider Foundation, World Wildlife Fund, etc.).

1.4. Problematic

Until recently, studies of outdoor activities have mainly considered the ecological and socioeconomic impact of these activities, with the goal being to understand tourism and suggest its harmonious development in different parts of the world (Bourdeau, Corneloup & Mao, 2002; Buckley, 2002). They have been conducted by economists for the most part, as have most works on sustainable development. In general, the various professionals are questioned about their organisations and relationships with other entities of the sporting structure (federations, committees, etc.) and economic partners (transportation, tourist accommodations, and so on, as shown by Bessy & Naria, 2004).

Most studies have assumed that outdoor activities contribute to the sustainable development of an area; some, however, have highlighted the negative ecological impact of these activities (Mounet, 2007). Very few have focused on professional outdoor instructors and their ethical problems. Yet, these frontline actors are most concerned by the contradictions in outdoor activities and their potential self-destruction.

Moreover, these professionals are the major educators and transmitters of ecological awareness. At least, this is often the message put forward by sporting institutions. What in fact do they really transmit to their clients?

This study aimed to better understand their professional practices and to specify their roles with regard to sustaining the natural environment. It is in line with the work of Corneloup and Bourdeau (2002), who highlighted the loss of a culture of professional nature enthusiasts because of economic trends. Our study thus aimed to analyse how they reason and the relationships they establish between their activity, nature and sustainable development.

2. Method

2.1. Participants

The participants were nine professional mountain guides from Mercantour National Park in the southern Alps, France. This profession was particularly interesting for a first study as mountain guides assist with the 'purest' outdoor activity, in the sense that walking is a 'natural' and 'simple' activity which is sparsely mediated by technical devices (contrary to surfing, rafting or mountain biking, for example). This group was quite representative of the entire mountain guide community in the southern French Alps in terms of age range (from 28 to 50 years old) and work status (self-employed, public-sector employees [university and municipal], and private-sector employees [of tour operators and holidays camps]). In addition, few actually lived in the mountains but instead lived in towns close to the waterfront (the Mediterranean), which is generally the case in this area. There were two women and seven men, which means that women were slightly over-represented in this sample (28%) compared to their proportion in the Mercantour National Park as a whole (16%).

2.2. Procedure

2.2.1. Interview guide. The interview guide was developed to help the participants describe their representations[5] of their professional activity, their thoughts about sustainable development, and their relationship with nature. The first section contained questions related to their work (e.g. How would you describe a good mountain guide? What are the main responsibilities? What are the values you want to transmit? What about environmental awareness?). The questions about sustainable development and nature in sections 2 and 3 were more open-ended (e.g. How would you describe sustainable development? What are the spontaneous ideas or images that the word 'nature' brings to mind?). These sections were non-directive to reflect the exploratory phase of this investigation. Throughout the interview, follow-up questions were used to help the participants to expand on and justify their responses.

2.2.2. Interviewer and interview procedure. The same interviewer conducted all the interviews in this study. He was a researcher in sports-oriented social psychology and was familiar with qualitative methods (Patton, 1990). Two pilot interviews were conducted, and minor refinements were made as a result of the participants' feedback.

After personal consent was given, individual interviews were conducted, with each lasting approximately 45 minutes. The interviews began with a presentation of the study, introductory comments and scientific precautions. All participants were assured that their identities would remain anonymous and that their personal opinions were important. The researcher then asked permission to record the interview. After the participants agreed to the request, the interviews started. They ended by asking the participants to share their perceptions of the interview and inviting them to make any additional comments.

2.2.3. Trustworthiness. Several methods were used to enhance the trustworthiness of the data. First, the pilot study helped to establish a conceptually aligned interview guide. Second, the interviews were audio-taped and transcribed verbatim. Further methods to ensure the trustworthiness of the analyses are described below.

2.2.4. Data analysis. Our thematic analysis was mostly inductive as the study was exploratory (Patton, 1990; Tesch, 1990). Raw data themes were first established based on the meaning units highlighted in the participants' responses (e.g. naturalist, historical and cultural information). The highlighted raw data themes were then classified into lower-order themes in relation to the domain they referred to (e.g. knowledge transmission). Finally, the lower-order themes were categorised in accordance with the main dimensions of the theme being dealt with (e.g. pedagogical dimension for the representations related to the job). The themes referred to the three themes of our study: the representations related to the profession of mountain guiding, sustainable development and nature.

The trustworthiness of this analysis was tested through investigator triangulation, which consisted of coding the data independently and then comparing and discussing the codes until a consensus was reached. Divergences in categorisation were discussed until consensus was reached (Lincoln & Guba, 1985).

3. Results

The thematic analysis of the entire set of interviews revealed that, despite the heterogeneity of the participants (in terms of status and sectors of activity: holidays, education, etc.), their representations about the profession, sustainable development and nature were quite homogeneous.

3.1. Mountain guides' representations of their professional activity

From a general point of view, being a mountain guide was seen as a work of 'passion' in which the borders between work, home life and self were often hard to distinguish. It seemed that these guides deeply identified with their work. This was the case for all interviewees, as illustrated by the following remarks:

> Doing this job is also a state of mind. It is a part of my family roots. (John)[6]

> Trekking is a philosophy. (Eric)

> We're not rolling in money but it's a way of life. (Suzy)

As noted in this last remark, the profession is not well paid and this was noted as an important factor, as seen in Table 1.

Table 1. Representations of the job

Dimensions	Themes	Second-order themes
Economic	The need to widen the range of sport and tourism products (o = 52, n = 9)*	
	Economic difficulties (o = 28, n = 9)	
Perceptions of client expectations	Expectation in terms of comfort (o = 45, n = 9)	
	Expectations in terms of knowledge (o = 51, n = 9)	
	Social and psychological expectations (o = 32, n = 9)	
	Hedonist expectations (o = 30, n = 9)	
	Immersion in a natural environment (o = 18, n = 9)	
Pedagogical	Knowledge transmission	Naturalist, historical and cultural information (o = 91, n = 9)
		Protection (o = 55, n = 9)
	Relational skills (o = 61, n = 9)	
	Didactic skills (o = 16, n = 7)	
	Technical abilities (o = 29, n = 9)	
	Pleasure transmission (o = 19, n = 8)	
Legal	Legal responsibility related to risks and safety (o = 67, n = 9)	
Communication	External communication	
	Advertisement (o = 12, n = 6)	
	Tourism Partners (o = 37, n = 9)	

(Continued)

Table 1. (*Continued*)

Dimensions	Themes	Second-order themes
	National Park	Positive image of the Park from a commercial point of view (o = 23, n = 9) Protection (o = 79, n = 9) Partnership (o = 27, n = 9) Critics (o = 16, n = 7)

Notes: * 'o' refers to the occurrences of the themes across all the interviews; 'n' refers to the number of participants who talked about this theme.

The poor pay is part of the precariousness of this profession and has prompted many mountain guides to constantly adapt their 'product' to the expectations and physical abilities of their clients. The activities involved in being a mountain guide have thus changed in recent years from the original long mountain treks to the day-long hiking trips of today and even simple walks, as noted by this young mountain guide:

> I found a book from 1988 in my village: the treks were two or three times as long and hard as they are today. They were for people who were experienced. (Peter)

This last remark underlines the growing democratisation of the practice of mountain guiding, which requires a continual remodelling of the job. Nowadays, there is an increasing expectation by clients of *comfort* in the associated facilities, as illustrated by the following remarks:

> The clients come for the nature, but they want it to be under control. Today, we often need to have help along to carry their belongings. (Jess)

> When the clients get to a shelter, they want it to be a three-star hotel. (John)

> Sometimes, we should even control the weather! (Fred)

In addition there are other expectations: about the guide's *knowledge* (of the environment, the flora and fauna, the culture and history of the area), about *social* opportunities (people come to be part of a group, to talk and sometimes even to confide in others), and about getting away from routines and being recharged.

Given the weight of these expectations, a considerable part of the mountain guide's job is *pedagogical*. As shown in Table 1, this dimension requires several abilities, the two most important being the *transmission of knowledge* and *relational skills* (according to the interviewees). The *transmission of knowledge* occurs at two levels: at a purely *informational* level and at a level that attempts to *protect* nature, as highlighted in the following quotes:

> We teach them about the world around them […] We try to interest them in how plants function, what an ecosystem is, anything that may work to get them interested. (Julian)

> We show them natural elements while talking about their vulnerability (Suzy).

Secondly, mountain guides work to develop healthy group dynamics and an atmosphere of conviviality in order to secure the loyalty of the clients:

> Often, people come back because they really like the guide. (Jess)

> These relationships may often lead to friendships. (Eric)

> We must take care of people. (Fred)

Given the constant need to adapt to the clientele, *didactic skills* seem to be expected so that 'hiking can be adapted to everybody's level' (Suzy) and the guides feel the need to anticipate any eventuality at any time. *Technical abilities* are added to knowledge of the environment and the activity (especially in terms of safety, equipment, etc.). Beyond these practical aspects, clients want to enjoy themselves while hiking. Mountain guides help them to experience their 'love for nature' so that they too can 'absorb it'. In fact, the outdoor activities professionals of the twenty-first century are both managers of tourist services and animators of sporting activities.

Another important aspect of the work of mountain guides is their *legal* (civil and criminal) *responsibility* in the case of an incident or accident. This dimension of responsibility was mentioned unanimously:

> A heavy load, especially since people have become litigious. (Eric)

> We can't play around with safety. (Julian)

> We can't forget that we can be taken to court at any time if we make a mistake. (John)

The last representations associated with the profession were related to *internal and external communication* and promotion. External promotion refers to *advertising*. Internal communication emerged as more important in terms of making their sport and the products associated with tourism visible and referred to all the networks established around the profession, especially *tourist partners* (tour operators, holiday camps, accommodation, etc.) and the Mercantour National Park, a guarantee in itself of the quality of the natural setting. This park is indeed well recognised as the 'idyllic' setting of many dreams. Moreover, most of the mountain guides thought that good management of a natural setting implies the participation of all involved: inhabitants, workers, and so on. The idea expressed was thus to protect both nature and the people who live or work there. These are the pillars of sustainable development that we next analysed.

3.2. Mountain guides' representations of sustainable development

As shown in Table 2, the representations related to sustainable development were numerous, heterogeneous and sometimes contradictory.

The mountain guides' most frequently expressed representation about sustainable development was *scepticism*. In fact, they are not at all convinced about the 'purity' of the goal, nor the means to achieve it. They noted that the idea of sustainability is often used for political or economic ends, as illustrated in the following excerpts from the interviews:

> For me, sustainable development is only a political and economic thing. (Bill)

> We know the problems but we don't respond to them. (Peter)

Table 2. Representations related to sustainable development

Themes	Second-order themes
Scepticism (o = 66), (n = 9)	
Current trends preventing sustainable development	Economic (o = 30, n = 8)
	Spatio-temporal (o = 5, n = 3)
Modes of transportation management (o = 22, n = 9)	
Waste management (o = 30, n = 9)	
Energy management (o = 18, n = 9)	
Local consumption (o = 26, n = 9)	
Small shops and producers (o = 14, n = 7)	
'Organic' foods (o = 3, n = 2)	
Means of evolving towards sustainable development	Experiences in nature (o = 31, n = 7)
	Holistic vision (o = 20, n = 5)
	Past vision (against progress) (o = 12, n = 9)
	Condemnation of some places for exploitation (o = 19, n = 6)
	Wilderness (o = 16, n = 8)
	Alternation in the exploitation of natural spots (o = 11, n = 5)
	Vulnerability (o = 5, n = 3)

Table 3. Representations related to nature

Themes	Second-order themes
Confusion being—nature (o = 23, n = 8)	
Mother Nature, Gaïa (o = 57, n = 9)	
'One must deserve nature' (o = 22, n = 7)	
Free environment (o = 35, n = 9)	
Biodiversity (o = 21, n = 9)	
Object of exploitation	Source of income (o = 12, n = 6)
	Playground (o = 10, n = 5)

> To me, sustainable development is like 'organic' products: bring it up wherever we can because it sounds good! (Fred)

These excerpts highlight the mountain guides' conviction that ideological and *financial stakes* often underlie the discourse on sustainability. They were also obstacles to be confronted on a daily basis. Although the main principles of sustainability had been understood and internalised by all the guides, today's lifestyles did not enable them to apply them:

> Sometimes, you're stuck: you have to buy something but you don't have much money, so you go for the Chinese product! (Joe)

> We move around a lot because of the nature of our work; so what should we do about transportation? (Bill)

> Here, nothing is organised for sustainable development. (Jess)

Transportation was indeed one of the most frequently mentioned themes associated with sustainable development, as well as *waste management*, *energy management* (water, electricity, and so on) and the *consumption of local foods* from *small shops and producers*. Once again, the current modes for regulating the economy were questioned, as expressed in the following remarks:

> On our way back from Jura, we saw a truck on the highway that was carrying cattle from Poland even though France is overproducing meat; there I said to myself: nothing makes sense anymore. (Eric)

> Sustainable development means eating local foods bought from small producers. Then the other food networks, which are always creating more and more needs among the population, will either fail or have to adapt. (Peter)

From a general point of view, ecological awareness has grown, especially among the young. According to the mountain guides, it will continue to develop thanks to a 'reintroduction' of humans into nature; that is to say, through *experience*, as suggested below:

> For kids, it's normal to eat tomatoes all year long; they can't understand because there are always tomatoes at the supermarket! [...] With us, in the ecopark, young people will face the environment and its seasons: they will see for themselves what can grow and what can't. (Bill)

Finally, some mountain guides expanded the notion of sustainable development to a global, *holistic vision* of humans as the source of every development around them, as expressed below:

> Sustainable development starts with respect for and knowledge of oneself and others, and then of the environment we live in, whether in towns or the countryside. (Joe)

This attempt to reunify humans with the natural world appeared even more in their representations of nature, as we will now show.

3.3. Mountain guides' representations of nature

The representations related to nature were characterised by the strong desire to see humans reunited with the natural world, possibly in reaction to the increasingly complex and artificial world that technology has created. The following excerpts underline this point explicitly:

> For me, it's a complete immersion [...] we're part of it, we're inseparable [...] we are as linked to this plant fibre here as we are to what we are today. (Eric)

> There are many psychological troubles that come from the separation between human beings and nature; it is important if we can help them to reconstruct this link (Suzy).

In fact, the mountain guides expressed an unlimited 'admiration' for nature as the object of and place for 'meditation' and 'contemplation'. A striking respect for *Mother Nature* and humility was expressed:

> Nature imposes its strength to man. (Bill)

> To me, nature is a religion. I live thanks to it. When I'm having a hard time, I go and seek refuge there. (Julian)

> I don't believe in God or anything else, but there is still something of the divine in nature. (Jess)

As a consequence of this transcendent respect, the guides expressed the belief that it takes effort to 'meet' nature: 'nature is something that *must be deserved*'. They also thought it important that nature remain *free* from human interference, especially regarding accessibility. This would preserve natural *biodiversity*, which was the real focus of the enchantment expressed by these professionals.

However, nature also represented a *source of income* for these men and women and it has become a genuine economic sector, which sometimes put them in uncomfortable situations from ethical and ecological perspectives and even with respect to their own identity, as we shall now highlight in our discussion.

4. Discussion

This study is concerned with the representations of mountain guides concerning their work and the way they articulate these representations with their conceptions of sustainable development and nature. The discussion will try to link these elements around the notion of responsibility.

When asked 'What are your responsibilities in your job?', 'responsibility' mainly and spontaneously had a legal meaning for the mountain guides. It is taken to imply obedience to the laws (or rules) of their community and some type of response to failure or transgression when necessary. Although this meaning dates from the nineteenth century (Schlegel, 2000), it has had a powerful impact on the mountain guides regarding the risks inherent in their professional activity. This meaning has persisted even though the notion of responsibility has expanded and been enriched by other considerations. We can assume that this first representation of responsibility was in part due to the emphasis on safety, both in the media and in training programmes for work in high-risk sports like trekking. Yet, as Vaillant (1995) stated, this first meaning of responsibility is 'pre-moral'. It does not refer at all to issues of autonomous behaviour or self-control.

It was only in response to other questions during the interviews that the mountain guides dealt with the issue of their responsibility for others (Levinas, 1969). This aspect of responsibility reflected their need to feel legally protected as they carried out their professional tasks, as well as their desire to adapt activities to the level and expectations of a wide range of clients. Indeed, beyond the need for legal protection, these professionals must constantly present their 'product' to clients and explain the decisions they make. This implies that they must be empathic and display great psychological dexterity as they explain their choice of itinerary or the cancellation of a hiking trip (because of bad weather forecasts or conflicts with hunters in the area, for example). As a mountain guide (Peter) emphasised, 'a "yes" never needs justification whereas a "no" requires a lot of explanation; having said that, we really have to learn to say "no" even if the clients are unhappy with it.' This is a situation when responsibility is most salient. As Etchegoyen noted (1999, pp. 159–161), 'the moral concept of responsibility is profoundly tested when contradictions appear […], in that very movement of decision making that brings us to dare to look at ourselves in a mirror. This moment in the decision is precisely the instant in which the others are the ones we are responsible for and who override all other stakes. An instant of disobedience, a decisive instant that separates the past from the future.'

The mountain guides operationalised their responsibility for the environment (Jonas, 1984) in different ways. First, the meaning of environmental responsibility was expressed through the great amount of quantitative and qualitative information transmitted to the clients concerning the natural world and how to protect it. However, the discourse about protection seemed to be limited in terms of sustainable development. Indeed, it concerned only the National Park rules about waste management and avoiding any destruction of natural spaces. But the mountain guides also tried to transmit their holistic and contemplative vision of Mother Nature, Gaïa, to their clients. As a consequence, they tried to 'immerse' their clients in the natural environment and make them feel a 'cosmic' unity, wherein human beings are just one of the 'elements' of nature. They thus went beyond the Cartesian and religious dualism that has set humans over nature, where humankind has become 'culture' in opposition to nature. Despite their submissive attitude towards nature and its dangers (cf. *The Leviathan* (Hobbes, 1651/1951)), which the mountain guides stressed, it was hard for them to pass on their unification message. In fact, with the invasion of technology in nearly every part of life today and our increasing attempts to dominate nature (e.g. through the artificial arrangement of pathways, with stairs cut into the mountains and even lifts on the steepest slopes), the guides reported finding it more and more difficult to encourage clients to adopt a poetic and contemplative approach to nature. This is what Atteia (2009) called 'the contemporary totalitarianism of technoscientism' when referring to the dictatorship of numbers and measurement to explain, transcribe, interpret and dominate reality. Yet this is what mountain guides often face in their discussions with clients about the gradient, the actual distance travelled, or their exact position thanks to GPS (brought along by these same clients). One mountain guide (Jo) reported that she sometimes felt like telling them: 'Stop it! Just enjoy the moment! Seize the day!' This fits with the perspective suggested by Bonnett (2002) on environmental education. Sensitising people to nature must also work through their sensations and emotions: learning is emotional as well as intellectual. This relates to the transcendental experiences of Thoreau (1854) and to the sensualist approach of Léopold (1949/1987, 'Think like a mountain'). Thus, some mountain guides assume that experience is the best way to learn and internalise environmental information, far superior to theoretical discourse on nature's vulnerability (which did not often emerge in the interviews). To them, responsibility is a praxiological morality.

However, mountain guides face two main difficulties. The first concerns the sustainability of their business activity and thus the need to satisfy their clients' desires and adjust to their capabilities. The monetary considerations attached to their business activities seemed to cause a real identity or philosophical crisis at times, especially because they considered their work to be a part of themselves. They were mountain guides by conviction. Consequently, they regularly 'toned down' their own emotional intensity regarding nature and accepted that that of their clients was not the same. This finding augments those of Corneloup and Bourdeau (2002) by specifying how these professionals risk losing their original identity and authentic relationships with nature, not only because of management necessities but also because of ethical considerations. According to Tap (1986), identity includes five dimensions: a temporal dimension, unity, a dynamic system of different identities (physical, psychological, social, professional, and so on), individuation and self-esteem. The first two dimensions refer to the continuity of identity and are thus relevant to our analysis. They embody the consistency of one's thoughts, principles and behaviour throughout one's life. In fact, mountain guides have often inherited their way of thinking and being towards nature from their family. This primary socialisation has been reinforced by their professional socialisation through which they have internalised a set of ideal ecological values. From the guides' biographical backgrounds, it is clear that they generally undergo training in the sports world federal organisations, which convey ideals. Beliefs developed through institutional socialisation are expressed primarily in the register of morals and a vision of ideal society (Ardoino, 1981). The guides' demonstration of their environmental values, their sense of the meaningfulness of nature, and their hopes is rewarded by social status in the eyes of the participants. We believe that a link exists between the guides' level of institutional socialisation through their federal practice and training and their display of environmental awareness. The opinions, beliefs, morals, customs, symbols and ways of thinking, developed through the institutional process of socialisation, are acquired through social norms, rites and practices within their professional context. The effects of this socialisation process are observed through the guides' level of commitment to the environmental values promoted by the profession, and through their level of respect for these values (Massiera, 2006). These shared—and displayed—values are the basis of their belonging to a specific social group among outdoor activities' instructors. They are also what give sense to their activity and their involvement in the protection of nature. Mountain guides embody this responsibility for environmental protection—this environmental responsibility—from the standpoint of identity. As a consequence, when the guides are obliged (because it is their livelihood) to take along people who are simply looking to have a good time in a natural setting without necessarily taking care of it, they encounter cognitive dissonance. Their behaviour and their values no longer match. We could say that this situation leads them to experience a 'floating identity' or an 'in-between identity'. Like anyone, in order to reduce this dissonant effect, they try to legitimate their behaviour *a posteriori*. By rewording their acts, they can manage to morally justify and accept them (Bandura, Barbaranelli, Caprara & Pastorelli, 1996)—in this case, from an ecological perspective. If ever the tension due to these moral dilemmas becomes too strong, they face two possibilities: abandoning some of their values or quitting their job.

The second difficulty mountain guides face concerns us all: the definition, tenets and ultimate goals of an imprecise concept—sustainable development. The mountain guides expressed strong scepticism about this concept. They believe that this term hides political and economic motives that in no way reflect a sense of responsibility for the environment. It illustrates the current cynicism, just like the 'organic' label: 'a real swindle' (John). When they spoke about sustainable development as they perceived it, their speech was hesitant and sometimes contradictory, as if solutions cannot be proposed without confronting all the trends of the modern world (demographic and economic trends, for example). This representational instability related to sustainable development in our opinion reflects both the fact that this concept was first developed in the political sphere before being conceptualised in the intellectual domain (Godard,

1994), and the fact that it may be an *aporia* in itself in the actual socioeconomic system.

Conclusion

The aim of this study was to interrelate the mountain guides' representations of their professional activity, sustainable development and nature. The findings highlight the contradictions between the way they would like to do their job and their clients' expectations. Indeed, they would like to sensitise people to the enchantment of nature, whereas most clients come to simply enjoy themselves and 'to consume nature as they would any other form of entertainment'. This ideological gap between their clients and themselves is sometimes painful for these outdoor activities professionals. Another contradiction also emerged from this study: how can mountain guides combine the development of their professional activity with the protection of nature? The difficulty of answering this question became clear with regard to sustainable development. How can a society develop economically while preserving its natural resources? The mountain guides were very sceptical about what they had heard about sustainable development, which is a consequence of its broad, imprecise and theoretical definition. This finding is of major importance because if people do not know what to think about sustainable development, they will not adopt ecologically aware conduct. This is the upcoming concern highlighted in environmental psychology (Weiss & Girandola, 2010).

The issues and dilemmas experienced by mountain guides in this study may be compared with those of people concerned with moral education as it seems that the tensions between moral ideals and sensitivity towards nature, and the realities of modern life that they encounter is a nice example of a broad phenomenon to which moral educators need to respond. Indeed, they often have to face contradictions between the values they want to transmit and embody and the current social reality and functioning. This tension is highlighted in Lipovetsky's book (2006) on 'paradoxical happiness', which underlines the prevalence of fast consumption over a more sensitive, humanistic and existential attitude towards nature and people within a 'hyper-consumption society' as this author calls it. As a consequence, the main question an educator has to face is the following: 'Shall I educate future consumers or 'responsible citizens', even if they are thereby removed from the actual social mainstream?'

Despite the limitations of our study (due to the small sample), it suggests many research perspectives in a variety of fields. First, it would be interesting to enlarge the sample to other outdoor activities professionals (such as mountain biking coaches, canyoning and climbing instructors, etc.) to analyse their representations of their activities in relation to sustainable development. We could then compare them in relation to their respective characteristics (for example, in terms of equipment which might maintain a distance from nature). We would then have more data to determine whether outdoor activities encourage environmental awareness or not; in fact, these activities could also be another way to exploit nature (which would then be associated with a new product of consumption and no longer a natural element). Second, from a broader point of view, it now seems urgent to determine what sustainable development means to people in general so that we can turn our attention to developing concrete and practical responses.

Acknowledgements

This study was supported by an ALCOTRA grant from the European Commission and the Mercantour French National Park. We are grateful to the mountain guides for their participation. We are also very grateful to Laura Schuft for her help in the translation and for her comments.

Notes

1. See the Olympic Charter, available online at: http://www.olympic.org/Documents/olympic_charter_en.pdf
2. See *Achieving the objectives of the United Nations through sport*: available online at: http://www.jaimehaiti.org/sportanddev.pdf
3. See http://www.britannica.com/bps/search?query=development
4. Quotations from French texts and from interview participants have been translated by the authors of this article.
5. In this article, the word 'representations' is used in the sense of 'social representations', a concept first developed in France by Moscovici (1961). Social representations are defined as a system of ideas, values and beliefs about something, an object (such as 'nature', 'sustainable development' or 'a job'). They are built individually and socially at the same time since each person develops whilst having particular experiences in specific social environments. As a result, social representations have several functions, according to Abric (1994): a knowledge function (they enable people to explain the world in which they live); an identity function (they illustrate the identity of the groups to which an individual belongs and their values); an orientation function (they guide people's behaviour); and a justification function (they enable people to rationalise their conduct *a posteriori*).
6. The names used in this article are fictitious.

References

Abric, J-C. (1994). *Pratiques sociales et représentations* [Social practices and representation]. Paris: Presses Universitaires de France.

Appel, K.O. (1993). La crise écologique en tant que problème pour l'éthique du discours [Ecological crisis as a problem for discourse ethics]. In G. Hottois & M.G. Pinsart (Eds.), *Hans Jonas: Nature et responsabilité* [Hans Jonas: Nature and responsibility] (pp. 94–130). Paris: Vrin.

Ardoino, J. (1981). *L'intervention institutionnelle* [Institutional intervention]. Paris: Payot.

Arnold, P.J. (1997). *Sport, ethics and education*. London: Cassell.

Atteia, M. (2009). *Le technoscientisme, le totalitarisme contemporain* [Technoscientism, the contemporary totalitarism]. Gap: Editions Yves Michel.

Ballet, J., Dubois, J-L., & Mahieu, F-R. (2004). A la recherche du développement socialement durable: concepts fondamentaux et principes de base [In search of socially sustainable development: fundamental concepts and basic principles]. *Développement durable et territoires*, Dossier no. 3, Lille, 2004. Available online at: http://developpementdurable.revues.org/107 (accessed 18 April 2012).

Bandura, A., Barbaranelli, C., Caprara, G.V., & Pastorelli, C. (1996). Mechanisms of moral disengagement in the exercise of moral agency. *Journal of Personality and Social Psychology, 71* (2), 364–374.

Bazin, D. (2007). *Sauvegarder la nature – Une introduction au principe responsabilité de Hans Jonas [Protecting nature – An introduction to Hans Jonas's imperative responsibility]*. Paris: Editions Ellipses.

Bessy, O., & Naria, O. (2004). Les enjeux des loisirs et du tourisme sportif de nature dans le développement durable à l'île de La Réunion [The issues of recreation and sports tourism in sustainable development on the island of Réunion]. In P. Bouchet & C. Sobry (Eds.), *Management et marketing du sport: Du local au global [Management and marketing of sport: From the local to the global]. Actes du 4ème Congrès de la Société Française de Management du Sport [Proceedings of the 4th Congress of the French Society of Sport Management]*, pp. 68–81. Villeneuve d'Ascq: Presses Universitaires du Septentrion.

Bonnett, M. (2002). Education for sustainability as a frame of mind. *Environmental Education Research, 8*(1), 9–20.

Bouhaouala, M., & Chifflet, P. (2001). Logiques d'actions des moniteurs des sports nature: Entre passion et profession [Outdoor instructors' strategies: Between passion and profession]. *Revue STAPS, 56*(3), 61–74.

Bourdeau, P., Corneloup, J., & Mao, P. (2002). Adventure sports and tourism in the French mountains. Dynamics of change and challenges for sustainable development. *Current Issues in Tourism, 5*(1), 22–32.

Bredemeier, B.J., & Shields, D. (1986). Athletic aggression: An issue of contextual morality. *Sociology of Sport Journal, 3*(1), 15–28.

Buckley, P.J. (2002). Is the international business research agenda running out of steam? *Journal of International Business Studies, 33*(2), 365–373.

Corneloup, J., & Bourdeau, Ph (2002). Culture professionnelle et métiers du tourisme sportif de montagne [Professional culture and outdoor sporting tourism]. *Revue Teoros, 20*(3), 32–44.

Elliot, J.A. (1999). *An introduction to sustainable development* (2nd edn). London: Routledge.

Etchegoyen, A. (1999). *La vraie morale se moque de la morale—Etre responsable* [True ethics pokes fun at ethics—Be responsible]. Paris: Editions du Seuil.

Godard, O. (1994). Le développement durable: paysage intellectuel [Sustainable development: intellectual basis]. *Natures, Sciences, Sociétés, 2*(4), 309–322.

Hobbes, T. (1651/1951). *Leviathan: Or matter, form and power of commonwealth, ecclesiastical and civil.* Oxford: Blackwell.

Jonas, H. (1984). *The imperative of responsibility: In search of an ethics for the technological age.* Chicago, IL: and London: University of Chicago Press.

Léopold, A. (1949/1987). *A Sand County almanac and sketches here and there.* New York, NY: Oxford University Press.

Levinas, E. (1969). *Totality and infinity: An essay on exteriority*, trans. A. Lingis. Pittsburg, PA: Duquesne University Press.

Lincoln, Y.S., & Guba, E.G. (1985). *Naturalistic inquiry.* Newbury Park, CA: Sage.

Lipovetsky, G. (2006). *Le bonheur paradoxal—Essai sur la société d'hyperconsommation* [Paradoxical happiness—Essay about the hyper-consumption society]. Paris: Editions Gallimard.

Long, T. (2008). *L'éducation par le sport: Imposture ou réalité?* [Education through sport practice. Fake or reality?]. Paris: Connaissances et Savoirs.

Long, T., Pantaléon, N., Bruant, G., & d'Arripe-Longueville, F. (2006). A qualitative study of moral reasoning of young elite athletes. *The Sport Psychologist, 20*, 330–347.

Loret, A. (1995). *Génération glisse* [Fun generation]. Paris: Autrement.

Massiera, B. (2006). La socialisation à l'oeuvre dans l'univers fédéral, élément déterminant de la régulation sociale de l'organisation sportive [Federal socialisation as a determining element of the social regulation of a sporting organisation]. *Communication, 24*(2), 131–140.

Moscovici, S. (1961). *La psychanalyse, son image et son public* [Psychoanalysis, its image and its audience]. Paris: Presses Universitaires de France.

Mounet, J-P., (2007). Sports de nature, développement durable et controverse environnementale [Outdoor sports, sustainable development and environmental controversy]. *Natures, Sciences et Sociétés, 15*(2), 162–167.

Mounet, J-P., Nicollet, J-P., & Rocheblave, M. (2000). L'impact des activités sportives de nature sur l'environnement naturel [The impact of outdoor activities on the natural environment]. Montagnes Méditerranéennes 11, Tourisme sportif et territoires. Available online at: http://jeanpierre.mounet.free.fr/Publicationstelecharger/Mounet%20Nicollet%20Rocheblave_2000.pdf (accessed 18 April 2012).

Patton, M.Q. (1990). *Qualitative evaluation and research methods*. London: Sage Publications.

Pezzey, J. (1989). Economic analysis of sustainable growth and sustainable development. *World Bank, Environment Department, Working Paper, 15*, 1058–1072.

Pociello, C. (1981). *Sport et société* [Sport and society]. Paris: Vigot.

Pociello, C. (1995). *Les cultures sportives* [Sport cultures]. Paris: Presses Universitaires de France.

Schlegel, J-L. (2000). *Evolution de la notion de responsabilité depuis 1950—Les jeunes et leur rapport au droit* [Changes in the notion of responsibility since 1950—Young people and their relationships to law]. Paris: Dossier documentaire issu des journées des 8 et 9 Novembre, 2000.

Tap, P. (1986). Personnalisation et intersubjectivité [Personalisation and intersubjectivity]. *Connexions, 47*, 149–164.

Tesch, R. (1990). *Qualitative research analysis types and software tools*. New York, NY: Falmer Press.

Thoreau, H.D. (1854). *Walden or life in the woods*. Princeton, NJ: Princeton University Press.

United Nations World Commission on Environment and Development (UNWCED). (1987). *Our common future* (The Brundtland Report). Oxford: Oxford University Press.

Vaillant, M. (1995). Droit à l'adolescence, droit à la clémence, droit à la responsabilité [Right to adolescence, right to tolerance, right to responsibility]. *Journal du Droit des Jeunes, 144*, 22–25.

Vignal, B., & Chazaud, P. (2001). Vers une prise en compte des rapports à la nature dans l'organisation des pratiques de plein air [Towards a consideration of relationships with nature in the organisation of outdoor activities]. 9th International Congress of Physical Activities, 1–3 November 2001, Valence, France.

Weiss, K., & Girandola, F. (2010). *Psychologie et développement durable* [Psychology and sustainable development]. Paris: Editions In Press.

Promoting ethical and environmental awareness in vulnerable communities: a research action plan

Ulisses Araújo
University of São Paulo, Brazil

Urban populations that live in the outskirts of major Latin American cities usually face conditions of vulnerability attached to complex environmental issues, such as the lack of sewerage, floods, pollution and soil and water contamination. This article reports an intervention research programme in São Paulo, Brazil that combines a moral education approach with sustainability awareness in vulnerable communities. The main conceptual foundations of the project, designed to empower the community and promote ethical and environmental awareness are: strengthening the ties between the school and the surrounding community in order to construct 'moral atmosphere'; adoption of Problem- and Project-based Learning and the Design Thinking approach to reach the proposed goals.

Introduction

This article presents an action plan, related to an intervention research project to be conducted in a public high school located in a poor area of the city of São Paulo (Brazil), one of biggest cities in the world with over 14 million inhabitants. Its starting point is an investigation undertaken between 2007 and 2008 in two Brazilian public schools. That research, published in the *Journal of Moral Education* (Araújo & Arantes, 2009) aimed, among other goals, to develop efficient tools to change the mindsets of young people towards the development of ethical awareness, understanding and reasoning in schools and communities.

From this former project, our research group[1] is beginning a new investigation focusing on moral education and urban environmental issues in the east of the city of São Paulo, an area with 4.5 million inhabitants and with the lowest Human Development Index[2] (HDI = 0.478) in the whole city. As is common in such poor and densely populated urban areas, there are complex environmental issues to be faced by the population and government agencies, such as the lack of sewerage, floods, pollution and soil and water contamination, combined with a high socially vulnerable population, characterised by low income and poor educational background. According to Alves (2006) around 40% of the population in São Paulo with high social vulnerability also live with high environmental vulnerability. The situation in the project area is consistent with that described by the Global Science Panel on Population Environment (IIASA, 2002):

> Many factors contribute to vulnerability, including poverty, poor health, low levels of education, gender inequality, lack of access to resources and services, and unfavorable geographic location. Populations that are socially disadvantaged or lack political voice are also at greater risk. Particularly vulnerable populations include the poorest, least empowered segments, especially women and children. Vulnerable populations have limited capacity to protect themselves from current and future environmental hazards, such as polluted air and water and catastrophes, and the adverse consequences of large-scale environmental change, such as land degradation, biodiversity loss, and climate change. (p. 3)

Human–environmental interaction is a key contemporary issue which is mobilising the whole world towards the search for sustainable development of local and global communities. According to Pandey (2001), it is widely understood that the well-being of human society, and each human being, is closely related to the well-being of natural ecosystems. In this respect, meeting the needs of present and future generations, aiming at the reduction of poverty and the conservation of the planet's life support systems are major challenges of what has become known as 'sustainability' (Kates, 2011). Insofar as pursuing such well-being and sustainability will unavoidably involve the expression of moral values and will provide ongoing practical situations for moral decision-making and enactment, it is clear that environmental and moral education will be deeply interwoven in the context of our project.

Empowering the community and the young people in the school setting to have a leading role in finding short- and long-term solutions for the complex environmental problems that they face in their daily lives, by adopting an ethical perspective of sustainability, is the overarching goal of the environmental education programme we are implementing in one public high school[3] in the eastern area of São Paulo.

This programme combines a moral education approach with sustainability awareness in vulnerable communities, adopting a perspective of complexity in which human–environmental interactions that support environmental education cannot be disconnected from moral education. This article presents the plan of an intervention research project that will try to evaluate the ethical and environmental awareness of students and the community, as well as possible changes in the local community due to this awareness.[4]

A moral and environmental education project

In this research project we assume as a theoretical reference Jean Piaget's constructivist and interactionist epistemological perspective (1967). From his conception of a radical constructivism (Von Glasersfeld, 1982, 1984), we can understand that values are not predetermined, as defended by sociobiologists, nor are they merely internalised (from outside), as defended by behaviourists; rather, they are constructed from the subject's actions towards the objective and the subjective world. This concept of an active subject is important in recognising that moral values are not (or at the least are not wholly) determined by genes, nor just shaped by society, culture and the environment in which people live, but also depend on actual interactions, experiences and reflections related to ethical issues.

Assuming this perspective and adopting a naturalistic approach, which tries to understand human constructions of reality in social contexts, designing a moral and environmental education programme that aims to foster the construction of ethical and environmental awareness, and also the transformation of the local communities and the empowerment of its participants, led us to consider many different methodological and pedagogical strategies, all of them putting an active subject in the centre of the learning process.

The main conceptual foundations of the project are: (a) strengthening the ties between the school and the surrounding community to construct 'moral atmosphere' (Araújo & Arantes, 2009; Brazil. Ministério da Educação, 2007; Narvaez, 2006; Power & Higgins-D'Alessandro, 2008;); (b) the methodological and epistemological perspective of Problem- and Project-based Learning (Barrows & Tamblyn, 1980; Graaff & Kolmos, 2007); and (c) the Design Thinking approach (Meinel & Leifer, 2011; IDEO, 2009). Each of these is explained below.

School and community

The concept of 'moral atmosphere', which evolved through Kohlberg's Just Community approach (Power, Higgins, & Kohlberg, 1989), has developed towards a more complex perspective in which the community as a whole (of which the school is a part) creates a climate—a culture of morality—in which each subject is embedded and surrounded by ethics and citizenship principles and actions (Araújo & Arantes, 2009; Brazil. Ministério da Educação, 2007; Power & Higgins-D'Alessandro, 2008). Narvaez (2006, p. 707) also points to the importance of the community in the development of moral personhood, saying that 'this is the essence of *eudaimonia* (flourishing). In this Aristotelian view, every individual actualizes virtues in self [*sic*] with the support necessary from friends, associates, and society as a whole'.

The School Forum of Ethics and Citizenship is a main strategy in this project to promote the relationship between school and community and empower them towards the construction of moral atmosphere. The Forum occurs once in a semester and is intended to involve teachers, students, staff, district school managers, businessmen, families, churches, non-governmental organisations (NGOs) and community members in the organisation and development of activities and projects related to ethics and citizenship themes (such as ethics, democratic coexistence, human rights and social inclusion), integrating the school and the nearby community in a project of moral education (Araújo & Arantes, 2009; Brazil. Ministério da Educação, 2007).

Brazilian schools have considerable experience in using this pedagogical and communitarian tool to promote active morality. It was a central element of the Ethics and Citizenship Programme, a moral education project developed by the Brazilian government to promote education in ethics and citizenship in Brazilian elementary, middle and high schools. The Programme was implemented by the Ministry of Education (MEC) in more than 2000 schools, all over the country, between 2003 and 2010 (Araújo & Arantes, 2009; Brazil. Ministério da Educação, 2007). As a special consultant to the MEC for this Programme, and being responsible for creating textbooks and the teacher training to set up the Programme, I closely followed several schools—many of them in vulnerable communities—in the implementation of the School Forum of Ethics and Citizenship, and observed its potential for creating moral awareness in young people (Araújo & Arantes, 2009).

The Forum's main goal is to define ethical themes that will be developed in classrooms and in the neighbourhood through cross-curricular projects. Although the teachers are not obliged to participate, it is a culmination of a discussion process in the school towards the definition of a general theme that will mobilise the school and the surrounding community in the months ahead.

In the Forum meeting lasting 2–3 hours an invited person (or a round table with three participants) initially presents general ideas about specific environmental issues that affect the nearby community. This is followed by a debate that aims to narrow down the theme to the school's and the community's needs and to set up some guidelines for the cross-curricular projects during the next term. Each participating teacher or the collective responsible for each class/grade[5] is responsible for creating the specific projects inspired by the Forum's decision, and for its subsequent development.

Possible topics, such as the lack of sewerage in the homes of the neighbourhood, the regular floods that affect the district because it is surrounded by the Tiete River, air pollution and soil and water contamination due to former and existing chemical industries in this urban area, may be explored in the communities participating in the project. It is hoped that reflecting and acting by means of cross-curricular projects related to these topics—which clearly have ethical components due to the programme's aim of improving the lives and well-being of peoples and their community—might foster the development of ethical and environmental awareness in the school and community participants.

Problem- and Project-based Learning

Nowadays, education in general is facing challenges that demand a change in the teaching–learning relationship, as well as in the role played by students and teachers at school. As some authors point out (e.g. Shulman, 2004; Weimer, 2002) the focus should move from a teaching perspective, where there is someone responsible to transmit knowledge to others, to a student-centred learning perspective, where students assume a participatory role in their apprenticeship and in the search for knowledge using active learning methods.

In this latter conception, education can be an intellectual adventure, mediated by teachers who allow students a voice, promote collective and cooperative learning experiences, encourage curiosity and give them conditions to find answers to their own questions about everyday life and scientific knowledge.

The Problem- and Project-based Learning approach is one of the main innovative active learning methodologies being implemented at all educational levels all around the world. According to Barrows and Tamblyn (1980), Problem-based Learning is a learning method based on the principle of using problems as a starting point for learning. Mayo, Donnely, Nash, and Schwartz (1993) say that Problem-based Learning is a pedagogical strategy for posing significant, contextualised, real-world situations, and providing resources, guidance and instruction to learners as they develop content knowledge and problem-solving skills. There is a variant of this conception, known as Project-based Learning. Graaff and Kolmos (2007), mentioning the Danish author Algreen-Ussing, define it as:

> A complex effort that necessitates an analysis of the target problem analysis and that must be planned and managed, because of desired changes that are to be carried out in people's surroundings, organization, knowledge, and attitude to life; it involves a new, not previously solved task or problem; it requires resources across traditional organizations and knowledge. (p. 4)

In this moral and environmental education programme we adopt the Problem- and Project-based Learning approach as core epistemological and methodological principles for involving students and the school community in project work that has a goal of building ethical and environmental awareness based on sustainability.

It is envisaged that changing the traditional school organisation of time and space will be necessary to attain this. With the local environmental theme defined by the School Forum of Ethics and Citizenship as a reference for the school term many curricular activities will be developed beyond the schools' walls in its neighbourhood.

Following a collective decision by the Forum, as a planned activity in the research, groups of students will study the problems caused by the regular floods of the Tiete River in the nearby community and how they affect people's lives. This is the general theme, and the specific problems to be studied will be raised by the students. Talking to their neighbours, observing the social, geographical and environmental contexts of the area, interviewing people to know the reasons why they keep living in those areas could be the raw material for the students in order to ask questions that will guide the cross-curricular projects. Different groups of these high school students will have differing and complementary problems to study and solve.

In this way, the projects will be driven by the problems raised by the students in contextualised real-world situations, connected to the local community needs in an ethical–sociopolitical perspective. The curricular change lies in the conception that the problems to be studied are not defined by the teachers, nor the principal or the school board. With reference to the Forum theme, students play an active role in the learning process and teachers must assume the role of mediation and guidance. The traditional school curriculum, of chemistry, geography, language, mathematics, biology and arts, is comprehended from a multidisciplinary and interdisciplinary perspective and used as a tool to understand the complexity of the ethical and environmental issues and to answer the students' and community's questions.

The Design Thinking approach

In our goal to construct ethical and environmental awareness based on sustainability, we have envisaged a process of finding innovative solutions to the community's needs, by involving all project participants in the search to overcome obstacles that prevent people's well-being and the construction of a community moral atmosphere.

Complementing the conceptual foundations of the programme, we are adopting the *Design Thinking* approach. According to Meinel and Leifer (2011), Design Thinking is a human-centric methodology that integrates multidisciplinary collaboration and iterative improvement to produce innovative products, systems and services with an end-user focus. It is human-centred because the process of designing innovative services begins by examining the needs, dreams and behaviour of the targeted people to be affected by the designed solutions, listening to and understanding them (IDEO, 2009).

We are using IDEO's[6] *Toolkit* (2009) as a resource in our project. Their Human-Centred Design Toolkit was designed specifically for NGOs and social enterprises that work with impoverished communities in Africa, Asia and Latin America, supporting them to understand a community's needs in new ways, find innovative solutions to meet those needs, and deliver solutions with sustainability in mind. Among solutions developed under this human-centred material, which involve university and community interaction, they cite CleanWell natural antibacterial products.

The process of Human-Centred Design Thinking starts with a challenge. In our project, this will be some aspect of the problem identified by the students, such as 'How can we improve the well-being and lives of people affected by the Tiete River floods?' The process is developed through three phases: hear, create and deliver (IDEO, 2009). Based on IDEO's *Toolkit*, during the Hear Phase student groups will collect stories and listen to the needs and desires of the people living in the neighbourhood. The Creation Phase consists in translating what was heard from people into frameworks, opportunities, solutions and prototypes of products, processes and policies thought to improve peoples' well-being. Finally, the Deliver Phase will analyse costs, capability assessment and implementation planning.

We believe that Human-Centred Design Thinking, which is an approach based on a problem- and project-based conceptualisation, is a way to empower the community, through creative and innovative processes, in the search for solutions for their own problems. In the specific situation of this programme, using ethical and environmental issues as tools to understand the community's needs and desires, it might help to empower the students who live in that area to work in a collaborative and cooperative way, aiming at overcoming vulnerability through the improvement of their own lives and that of the community.

Method

As a complex research project developed in a naturalistic setting, a multi-method approach will be adopted, in the belief that qualitative and quantitative methods would add breadth, depth and reliability, to the investigation (Denzin & Lincoln, 1994; Valles, 1999). Four main instruments, allowing qualitative and quantitative analysis, are planned to be used in the data collection:

- *semi-structured interviews* to be held with the school and community participants, before, during and after the intervention programme, with questions focusing on their perception of the local environmental issues they face and the approaches used to overcome them;
- *written reports* describing direct observations, informal conversations and the pacing of the actions implemented during the intervention programme;
- *portfolios* reporting the projects developed by the groups and the *design thinking* process; and
- *written questionnaires* to assess students' ethical and environmental awareness in which conflict-solving situations and open-ended questions will be presented to the school and community participants before and after the intervention programme. Here, we will try to capture their concerns and awareness regarding issues such as justice, solidarity, citizenship, the pursuit of personal and collective happiness, causes and consequences of local human–environmental interactions and the impact of the lack of sewerage, floods, air pollution, soil and water contamination in the community life.

Concluding remarks

For the intervention research project we are developing in a Brazilian public school, to empower community and promote ethical and environmental awareness in high school students, we have designed a moral education programme that articulates three main methodological strategies. First, the implementation of a School Forum of Ethics and Citizenship to integrate the school and the nearby community in the development of cross-curricular projects related to local environmental issues is an initial way to create a moral atmosphere that is intended to promote ethical and environmental awareness and empower community. Second, Problem- and Project-based Learning is a methodological and epistemological approach to involve students in an active learning role, giving new dimensions to the process of learning moral virtues and values, as well as to build awareness of the human–environmental interaction issues that affect the students' lives. Finally, we are adopting the perspective of Human-Centred Design Thinking to help the community in searching for creative and innovative ways to look for solutions for their own environmental problems.

With these strategies we aim to develop ethical and environmental awareness in school and in the nearby community. The ultimate goal is to create an embedded moral education approach that empowers students and the community where they live to overcome vulnerability from a sustainable perspective.

Notes

1. Centro Interdisciplinar de Pesquisas em Complexidade e Cidadania (CIPECC) [Interdisciplinary Research Center on Complexity and Citizenship].
2. An index created by the United Nations Development Programme (UNDP).
3. Brazilian high school students range from 15 to 18 years old.
4. In this article, ethical awareness represents consciousness of and a concern about values and virtues, such as justice, solidarity, citizenship and the pursuit of personal and collective happiness. Environmental awareness, in the same way, represents human–environmental interaction issues that affect the well-being of human society related to the well-being of natural ecosystems.
5. It is important to mention that participation in the Forum is not mandatory for the school teachers.
6. IDEO is a design consultancy firm located in Palo Alto (California) that takes a human-centred, design-based approach to helping organisations to be innovative.

References

Alves, H.P. (2006). Vulnerabilidade socioambiental na metrópole paulistana [Socio-environmental vulnerability in the metropolis of Sao Paulo]. *Revista Brasileira de Estudos Populacionais, 23*(1), 43–59.

Araujo, U., & Arantes, V. (2009). The Ethics and Citizenship Program: A Brazilian experience in moral education. *Journal of Moral Education, 38*(4), 489–511.

Barrows, H.S., & Tamblyn, R. (1980). *Problem-based learning: An approach to medical education.* New York, NY: Springer.

Brazil. Ministério da Educação [Ministry of Education]. (2007). *Programa Ética e Cidadania [Ethics and Citizenship Program]*. Brasília: Ministério da Educação.

Denzin, N.K., & Lincoln, Y. (Eds.). (1994). *Handbook of qualitative research.* Thousand Oaks, CA: Sage.

Graaff, E., & Kolmos, A. (2007). *Management of change—Implementation of Problem-Based and Project-Based Learning in Engineering.* Rotterdam, The Netherlands: Sense Publishers.

International Institute for Applied Systems Analysis (IIASA) (2002). *Global Science Panel on Population Environment—GSP: Analyses, goals, actions, realities.* Available online at: http://www.iiasa.ac.at/gsp/ (accessed 18 March 2011).

IDEO (2009). *Human-Centered Design Toolkit.* Available online at: http://www.ideo.com/work/human-centered-design-toolkit (accessed 18 March 2011).

Kates, R.W. (2011). What kind of a science is sustainability science? *Proceedings of the National Academy of Sciences, 108*(49), 19,449–19,450.

Mayo, P., Donnely, M.B., Nash, P.P., & Schwartz, R.W. (1993). Student perceptions of tutor effectiveness in problem-based surgery clerkship. *Teaching and Learning in Medicine, 5*(4), 227–233.

Meinel, C., & Leifer, L. (2011). *Design thinking: Understand, improve, apply*. Berlin: Springer.

Narvaez, D. (2006). Integrative ethical education. In M. Killen & J. Smetana (Eds.), *Handbook of moral development* (pp. 703–733). Mahwah, NJ: Erlbaum.

Pandey, D.N. (2001). *Sustainability science of local communities*. Available online at: http://www.sciencemag.org/cgi/eletters/292/5517/641 (accessed 6 February 2012).

Piaget, J. (1967). *Biologie et connaissance [Biology and knowledge]*. Paris: Editions Gallimard.

Power, F.C., & Higgins-D'Alessandro, A. (2008). The just community approach to moral education and the moral atmosphere of the school. In L. Nucci & D. Narvaez (Eds.), *Handbook of moral and character education*. New York, NY: Routledge.

Power, C., Higgins, A., & Kohlberg, L. (1989). *Lawrence Kohlberg's approach to moral education*. New York, NY: Columbia University Press.

Shulman, L.S. (2004). *The wisdom of practice*. San Francisco, CA: Jossey-Bass.

Valles, M.S. (1999). *Técnicas cualitativas de investigación social, reflexión metodológica y práctica profesional [Qualitative techniques of social investigation, methodological reflection and professional practice]*. Barcelona: Editorial Síntesis Sociologia Ltda.

Von Glasersfeld, E. (1982). An interpretation of Piaget's constructivism. *Revue Internationale de Philosophie, 36*(4), 612–635.

Von Glasersfeld, E. (1984). An introduction to radical constructivism. In P. Watzlawick (Ed.), *The invented reality* (pp. 17–40). New York, NY: Norton.

Weimer, M. (2002). *Learner-centered teaching*. San Francisco, CA: Jossey-Bass.

Like a swallow, moving forward in circles: on the future dimension of environmental care and education

Dirk Willem Postma[a] and Paul Smeyers[b]

[a]*University of Applied Sciences Utrecht, The Netherlands;* [b]*Ghent University and K.U. Leuven, Belgium*

After the moral framework of sustainable development, the focus on climate change appears to take a lead in the practice and theory of environmental education. Inherent in this perspective is an apocalyptic message: if we do not rapidly change our use of energy resources, we will severely harm the life conditions of our children and grandchildren. In this article we argue that environmental educators should liberate us from this highly instrumental dictate by taking their cue from our daily care for our environment as revealed in child's play in nature. Inherent in the interaction of the *Homo ludens* with nature is a spiral time experience. This time condition elicits a particular responsibility: rather than calculating which means are necessary to prevent future disasters, we should respond with care to the concentric circles of an open and indefinite future. Therefore, environmental education should not aim to prevent future disasters, but foster anticipating care for nature.

> We find ourselves at the center of concentric circles of caring. (Noddings, 1984, p. 46)

Education on behalf of future generations?

Despite all the controversy about what environmental education ought to be for and about, the participants in public discourse on environmental education would agree that it should prepare children for the practice of environmental citizenship. And not withstanding the debate about what this practice may imply, the participants surely agree that environmental citizenship involves responsibilities for the present-day situation as well as for the environment in which future generations will find themselves. The imperative of responding to future needs is thus recognised. One cannot remain indifferent, so it is argued, to the demands that future people make on us here and now, as they will inherit the world we leave behind. Our sense of justice requires us to consider the implications and consequences of what we do now for the quality of future life on this globe. This moral ideal is also at work in the public debate at large where similar intuitions seem to guide what is referred to as 'common sense'. In slogans and phrases used by political parties, for instance, future generations or 'our great-grand children' are often appealed to as an incentive for change. Furthermore, the biblical metaphor of 'stewardship' contains a clear notion of responsibility stretching out over several succeeding generations. The most influential articulation of intergenerational responsibility is perhaps offered by the international key concept of 'sustainable development', defining 'a development that meets the needs of the present without compromising the ability of future generations to meet their own needs' (United Nations World Commission on Environment and Development (UNWCED), 1987, p. 43). More recently, the paradigm of climate change has engendered a whole series of behavioural predicates such as 'climate neutrality', 'carbon neutrality', and the 'net zero carbon footprint'.

When environmentalists, scientists and politicians speak on behalf of future generations they refer not only to our children, grandchildren and great-grandchildren, but to all those yet unknown who will live in the future. Clearly, one cannot be sure but only surmise what it is that these human beings, who will live centuries from now, may desire. But taking up this kind of broadened responsibility, as well in terms of scope as of magnitude, widens the radius of our actions. Thus it is no longer sufficient in the present context of rapid economic and scientific development, to stick to one's initial responsibility for those descendants for whom we care, as it is realised that our personal consumption and the use of technology will have an impact on the world and well-being of all those who will live in the future. For example, it becomes questionable whether our present use of nuclear energy is consistent with an imperative of intergenerational responsibility, for, as long as scientists cannot guarantee safe and sustainable storage of nuclear waste, we deliberately take huge risks for future generations who may suffer from leakage. The same can be argued with regard to human effected climate change that will probably harm the living conditions of human posterity, or the uncertain effects of genetic engineering on the 'health' of our ecosystem in the long run. Whereas the consequences of human behaviour used to be confined to a distance in time and space which might be scoped, right now the intended and unintended effects of our behaviour stretch into the indefinite future with a magnitude that seems unprecedented. Obviously, an adequate account of environmental citizenship has to respond to these changing conditions of human responsibility.

A shared commitment to an ethic of intergenerational responsibility provides environmental educators with a strong claim for environmental citizenship. Yet, as soon as we pose the question how we should consider future needs or include the 'voice' of future generations in our civil practices, we leave the common ground, which turns out to be weak and superficial, rather than firmly principled and narrowly circumscribed. There are different views on the nature of our relationship with future generations, each of them leading to different sets of ethical implications. Issues are, for instance, the kind of relationship we should have with future people and how this commits us to act on their behalf; but also, what it is exactly in this relationship that inspires us to take up responsibility; and moreover, what these responsibilities consist of and how far they reach. In previous work three possible views on this issue of intergenerational responsibility and citizenship were explored (see Postma, 2006).

First, the standard liberal view underlying the dominant understanding of the framework of sustainable development, that requires us to regard future generations as hypothetical fellow citizens, was investigated. According to this view, we should represent the needs of future generations in public discourse by acting *as if* they were present. Or more specifically, we are supposed to judge and act in line with an intergenerational contract of distributive justice that can count on the hypothetical consent of future generations. Thus, our community of justice is being extended into the indefinite future, and the conditional rights of future citizens are, in principle, equally important as the rights of contemporaries. In this way liberal contractualists have a strong case for intergenerational justice. However, one of us (Postma, 2006) argued that a principle of intergenerational justice cannot be justified within the liberal framework; it carries with it a presupposition which is not fulfilled because future generations are beyond the reach of our reciprocal relationships (in the narrow sense of hypothetical mutual agreement that liberal contract theories, such as that of John Rawls, require). Besides, it is unclear how such an abstract principle of intergenerational justice should motivate us to take up responsibility for the well-being of future generations.

The identification of fundamental flaws within the liberal view led to the exploration of the communitarian view on intergenerational responsibility. Communitarian ethicists suggest that we should treat future generations as heirs of our moral community. We are called on to contribute to their 'good' since future members of our community share our ideals and conceptions of the good life. After our death, they will continue the practices and projects we cared for and invested in during our life. Without trusting that future generations will carry on our traditions and pursue our ideals in the future, our life here and now would hardly be worth living. Thus, our relationship with future generations is understood and experienced in terms of extended community ties. Such an extension makes it possible to make obligations to posterity derived from the commitment and solidarity expected within the present community. Although the communitarian view offers an adequate answer to the problem of motivation, the responsibilities that it gives rise to remain limited to members of the community. Furthermore, this view rests on an inadequate vision of society. The late—or postmodern—societies we live in are characterised by moral pluralism, individual lifestyles and the absence of a shared view on the good life. Consequently, a communitarian ethic of obligations to posterity loses its grounds of application in contemporary societies. Lack of awareness of this problem is predominantly caused by the tendency of communitarians to express communality in terms of abstract values, rather than in terms of interlocking and sometimes mutually interfering narratives.

The fundamental flaws of the liberal view, together with the shortcomings of the communitarian view, force us to adopt an alternative understanding of future generations as imagined strangers. Although drawing on different sources, this will be called a neo-republican view of intergenerational responsibility. Within this view the main focus shifts from the alleged needs, wants and rights of future generations to our present desires, expectations and imagination of the future world that bind us together here and now. Since we do not know any future people from first-hand experience, we cannot possibly know what choices they would be inclined to make when confronted with the particular conflicts of interest, needs, ideals or moral dilemmas we face right now. Therefore, most judgement on our part as to what kind of world people in the future will like, what 'resources' they will need to survive and what 'goods' will make their life worthwhile, reflects what we like and what we think 'worthwhile' and 'good' in our present world. Every attempt to include the rights, needs or goods of future citizens throws us back upon our own devices as to what we value as 'necessary', 'liveable', 'inalienable' or 'dignified'. This does not mean that we do not have to consider the existence of future generations. On the contrary, we should imagine what kind of world *we* wish them to live in, rather than calculating what the interests of its inhabitants could possibly be. This kind of future responsibility does not arise from moral lessons but will emerge in the process of public debate and participation in the civil society itself (Postma, 2006).

Education for an open future

When it comes to the educational issue, there are huge differences of opinion among neo-republicans and civil society theorists. But what appears to unite them is the fundamental conviction that civil education should take place within the public sphere itself. The (re-)creation of citizenship is itself regarded as a core responsibility of the political community. Citizens are expected to organise their political life and structure their institutions in a way that sustains and preserves the public spirit and engagement in collective affairs of each and every (future) citizen (Van Gunsteren, 1992, p. 119). In line with this neo-republican perspective, environmental education should be understood as a particular kind of initiation into our civil practices; an initiation in which newcomers are gradually involved as fellow citizens, who help to shape these practices and are, *ipso facto*, gradually assuming co-responsibility for the continuity of our practices in the future.

The fundamental question remains whether environmental educators merely offer an appealing perspective on the future or treat their pupils as human material for the establishment of this future world. Derek R. Bell testifies to the latter by stating that the aim of environmental education ought to be to 'create a new generation of citizens who are greener than their parents' (Bell, 2004, p. 43). Does this claim do justice to the right of children to an open future horizon, or does it lead to a colonisation of our future in such a way that we deny new generations the opportunity to shape their own future world? Many philosophers of education warn against the utilisation of education as a means for creating some preconceived 'ideal society'. On the other hand, every educational act and judgement casts its shadows ahead. By acting in a particular way now, the educator commits herself and the child to doing something in the future.

In our view, this particular dilemma originates from the paradoxical nature of educational responsibility, as characterised by Hannah Arendt in her renowned paper 'The crisis in education' (1958). Educators bear a double responsibility, so she argues, one of which aims to preserve the child's openness and newness against the powers of the established world, whereas the other aims to protect the durable world against the potential recklessness of the new generation. These two responsibilities may come into conflict with each other:

> The responsibility for the development of the child is in a certain sense a responsibility against the world: the child requires special protection and care so that nothing destructive will happen to him from the world. But the world, too, needs protection to keep it from being overrun and destroyed by the onslaught of the new that bursts upon it with each new generation. (Arendt, 1958, p. 504)

This tension is prevalent in the practice of environmental education because here, in particular, both child and world are vulnerable to each other's powers. On the one hand, there is the promise of a new generation and the ability to think about worldly problems; on the other hand, there are the consumerist threats inherent in contemporary youth culture. In this sense, Arendt argues, education is and should be a conservative enterprise:

> Our hope always hangs on the new which every generation brings; but precisely because we can base our hope only on this, we destroy everything if we so try to control the new that we, the old, can dictate how it will look. Exactly for the sake of what is new and revolutionary in every child, education must be conservative; it must preserve this newness and introduce it as a new thing into an old world, which, however revolutionary its reactions may be, is always from the standpoint of the next generation, superannuated and close to destruction. (Arendt, 1958, p. 510)

In Arendt's view, educators stand in relation to the young as representatives of the present world for which they must assume responsibility even though they themselves did not make it, and even though they may, secretly or openly, wish it were other than it is. As such, educators must present an authentic picture of the world—in all its potential and with all its flaws—that is open to critique and change. Arendt therefore argues against those progressive educators who introduce the young into a desired world instead of the world we actually live in. It would be a big mistake to transform our picture of the world on behalf of the young as though our desired future were already a reality. For this reason, educators should not inculcate us with the ideal of a bright green future Ecotopia. Instead they are called upon to show what commits us to the present world. Environmental educators ought to familiarise children with the problems that threaten our common world as part of their introduction into that world. When educators refuse to take responsibility for these worldly problems, and take refuge in utopias, risks of indoctrination and manipulation lie in wait (Arendt, 1958).

Arendt refines her statement that education should be conservative by stressing that education should take place in 'the gap between past and future'. The present offers us a possible space in which to recollect and understand the past in a way that does not determine the future, but does throw an illuminating light on it, and fosters responsibility for the future. As representatives of the present world, educators mediate between the old and the young by balancing between that which is 'no longer' and that which is 'not yet', or, as Levinson notes: 'To teach in this gap is to take on the twofold task of introducing students into a world that precedes them, while preserving the possibility that students might undertake something new in relation to this world' (Levinson, 1997, p. 450). According to Levinson, this gap is not mainly to conserve and preserve the past, but occupies a provocative space as well, one which opens the possibility of interrupting social processes that appear fixed and inevitable.

Moving beyond the ethic of self-restraint

By setting limits to the satisfaction of our consumer needs, environmentalists have, willingly or unwillingly, contributed to the promotion of a morality of austerity and self-restraint, as if they want to say: all things in life that are pleasant, comfortable, tasty or exciting are bad for the environment and should therefore be subject to rigorous self-discipline. In particular, advocates of sustainable development tend to underline that, if we want to live a sustainable life, we have to deny ourselves the pleasures of consumption and control our unsustainable impulses and bad habits. After all, the ideal of a sustainable development sets limits to our present use of natural resources, in such a way that these limits are assumed to be attributable to individual consumer behaviour, as defined in our 'ecological footprint'. Consequently, we should be willing to make our 'shallow desires'—our desire for a long morning shower, for cheap meat and vegetables, or for frequent holidays by air—subordinate to our desire for a sustainable future. Here environmental responsibility is presented as the ability of self-discipline or self-restraint that allows us to resist the temptations of consumer culture.

In itself, this picture of environmental responsibility is recognisable and seems to be realistic, but a strong appeal to self-restraint and self-discipline fails to touch upon our intrinsic motivation. Instead it primarily trades on our controlling responses, fuelled by fear; fear for loss of the things we care for, fear for future catastrophes, fear for our survival or the survival of posterity, fear of falling short in the eyes of others, fear of losing control of our future action, and so on. This insight lead Jonas to acknowledge the 'heuristics of fear'; more precise and stronger than positive mental states like joy or desire, fear of specific future dangers points our attention to those vulnerable goods we really care about (Jonas, 1984, p. 27).

Many environmentalists have in fact gained support and credibility by sketching apocalyptic future scenarios. However, in the long term such a strategy has proven to be a dead end. The fact that in hindsight some of the darkest doom scenarios have appeared to be exaggerated has given some environmentalists the dubious image of being modern-day Cassandras; that is, prophets of doom to whom nobody listens anymore. Besides, trading on fear as an educational means to motivate children to act, think or judge in a particular way would imply a step back to the dark ages of puritan education, in which the awareness of hereditary debt and the fear of a punitive God were the pedagogical *Leitmotif*. Against the heuristics of fear, educational thinkers like Nel Noddings (1984) and Marjan Margadant-Van Arcken (1990) suggest that educators ought to connect to child-like play and care and joy in life in their moral appeal.

According to Kant's *Critique of judgement* (1790/1987), it is through our sensuous pleasure in beauty that we transcend the inner conflict between duty and inclination. The aesthetic experience of natural beauty allows us to move beyond our desire for self-discipline towards a personal striving for aesthetic self-creation, understood in terms of self-expression: the self as a work of art, as Foucault chooses to say (1984/1988, p. 214). This caring is of an aesthetic nature, in the sense that it is an experience of responding to something particular that appeals to us. In our caring we express a recognition of something that fulfils us in a particular way, and invites the response: 'When the other's reality becomes a possibility for me, I care' (Noddings, 1984, p. 14). As such, this appeal to environmental responsibility takes on the form of an invitation to express what we desire in our involvement with the natural world.

The ethical significance of child's play in nature

It seems common for children to experience nature as something to play with and play in. Apparently, nature appeals to their spontaneous responses of imaginative creativity. Thus, trees challenge children to climb in them, ditches invite them to build dams, sand to make castles out of them, the moon to lure werewolves, woods trigger children to play hide and seek, rabbits invite them to care for them and chestnuts to gather them and make funny creatures out of them. But nature does not merely appeal to responses of a noble kind. By the same token, animals sometimes release a kind of sadistic playfulness within children. Consider, for instance, how cruel children can be towards vulnerable animals—putting salt on snails, pulling off the legs of a spider, chasing cats—eager as they are to explore what it feels like to be superior and exercise power. Although we may question the moral quality of this behaviour, in these sadistic responses children continue to display an intrinsic involvement: the animals are tormented without any purpose, but 'just for fun'.

There seems to be no consensus among researchers in the field of education and developmental psychology on what play is mainly for and about. Moreover, we find it difficult to give one definition of child's play that covers the various dimensions of this phenomenon. Rather, various (partly overlapping) characteristics can be given. First, the characteristic of intrinsic motivation refers to the fact that an action is done for its own sake and not brought about by basic bodily needs or by external rules or social demands. Second, the activity of playing is pleasurable and enjoyable to the child. Third, the behaviour is non-literal, meaning that it has an 'as if' or pretend quality. Fourth, the variation in form and context that playing usually displays designates a responsive flexibility of action (Smith & Vollstedt, 1985). Apart from these main characteristics, there is attention to the dimensions of voluntariness, bodily immediacy, the degree of engrossment in the play, the peculiar joy in repetition, and the enchantment of reality (cf. Huizinga, 1971; Hutchison, 1998, pp. 104–105).

Careful phenomenological study of child play gives rise to the idea that children express within their play the fulfilment they find in an aesthetic involvement with nature that allows them to recognise (in a practical and immanent way) the intrinsic values and disvalues of nature: the intrinsically good, true, beautiful, exciting and comforting, as well as the intrinsically bad, false, hideous, cruel and sad in nature. Of particular interest within the context of environmental education is the magical 'animism' inherent in the child's play world. In particular, young children respond to nature in an empathically and anthropomorphic way, ascribing human-like emotions and desires to animals, plants and things. Nature triggers their imagination in a special way; organisms and things are involved in their play as if they were active and intentional beings. Pets are taken care of as if they were babies in need of parenting; trees moving in the dark before dawn are regarded as ghosts; sick flowers are being nurtured and spoken to as if they were patients; the holes in the sand on the beach are underground cities that have to be protected against the marching breakers that come rolling in. According to Margadant-Van Arcken (1990), who studied child play in nature, such a response is not an expression of animistic reasoning. Children, who display animistic responses in their play, do not necessarily assume that flowers have human-like feelings and that trees are bewitched. Rather, it is that their imagination allows them to express the appeal arising from their intimate involvement with nature in animistic behaviour (Margadant-Van Arcken, 1990, p. 149).

Some environmental philosophers suggest that anthropomorphism can be seen as inversely proportional to anthropocentrism (Bonnett, 2004; Lemaire, 2002). The imagination that allows us to recognise human-like intentional forces beyond ourselves literally pushes our 'selves' away from the centre of our world. Thus the assumption is the more one responds to these forces in an empathic way, the less narcissistic our desires, views and attitudes will be. Obviously, our suggestion is not to promote animistic reasoning in general. Rather, it is to reveal the ethical significance of child play in nature. According to an elaborate review of research literature on children's natural play, there is some qualitative and quantitative evidence supporting the thesis that 'playing in natural spaces supports children's attachments to their local environments' and 'builds an appreciation of natural systems and a sense of connectedness' (Lester & Maudsley, 2006, p. 44). Although more detailed qualitative educational research is necessary to sustain our particular thesis, the previous exploration provides us with strong reasons to assume that the kind of aesthetic involvement in nature that allows us to experience the intrinsic values of nature can be found in child play in a most spontaneous and imaginative form. Within child play educators recognise that they do not have to teach children to care for nature by means of value transmission. If they strive to initiate children in the multiform practices of environmental care and responsibility, educators only need to appeal to a playful-bodily responsiveness that is present in any child. Even in situations where children respond in a way that we tend to reject (responses of carelessness, neglect, waste, sadistic or cruel responses), educators can usually react by appealing to alternative sources of caring response, latently present in the child.

Spiral time and responsibility

Returning to the question of future responsibility, we find a particular time horizon in the experience of play. Playing children find themselves in a dense reality, where objective measures of time and space are deferred in favour of a singular order of things. The act of playing opens up a space of possibilities where at the same time disparate and discontinuous things can be 'perceived'. Past and future events can appear to playing children as if they were simultaneously happening, following their experience of an expanding present. Furthermore, the joy in repetition alludes to the experience of a recurring present. This time experience is neither like Nietzsche's Eternal Recurrence of the Same (Nietzsche, 1883–1885/1995, pp. 220–221)—that would be a dreadful experience—nor like the ancient concept of Eternal Return, referring to spiritual experiences of an original state of being. Here, the playful experience of time appears to be cyclic rather than linear. To be more specific, in child's play time appears to proceed spirally; children enjoy repetition because it does not take them back to where they came from, but the reiteration moves them forward; it transforms their former experience to a higher or deeper level. As such, this spiral time awareness may be taken to encompass vertical aspects of the cyclic time concept as well as horizontal aspects of linear time.

According to Maurice Merleau-Ponty, spiral time experience not only characterises child's play, but adult life-world experience as well—albeit in a moderate form:

> We have seen there is no natural time, if we understand thereby a time of things without subjectivity. There is, however, at least a generalized time, and this is what the common notion of time envisages. It is the perpetual reiteration of the sequence of past, present and future (…) This time is the time of our bodily functions, which like it, are cyclic, and it is also that of nature, with which we co-exist. (Merleau-Ponty, 1962, p. 453)

If our sense of spiral time, inherent to child's play and human life-world experience in general allows us to be close to the natural cycles of seasons, day and night, blossom and decay, then our understanding of future responsibility for nature should take its starting point from this spiral time experience instead of a uni-linear one. But what does this time condition imply for our uni-linear notions of responsibility? Obviously, it is not possible to give a full analysis of its implications here, but we would like to conclude our article by sketching some general outlines.

1. From causal accountability to responsive care

If we experience the course of time spirally instead of linearly, then our future appears to lose predictability and controllability. A causal notion of future responsibility in terms of being accountable for the foreseeable consequences of one's actions in the future therefore loses its ground of application. Of course, through our experience of causes and effects we know that certain actions have unavoidable consequences. Our future responsibility is causal in the sense that it may preclude certain acts of which we can predict with a high probability that they will harm other persons or living beings, but it is impossible to determine what a causal notion of responsibility compels us to do in a broader sense, because the range of possible consequences of our actions is usually too wide, all the more with respect to the distant future. Thus, a causal notion of future responsibility invites an imperative of precaution rather than care for the continuation of the things that make our life worth living. To move beyond the restrictive premises of predictability and controllability, it will be necessary to think of future responsibility as rooted in a caring responsiveness to the call of an open and indefinite future as described before.

On the other hand, cyclic time experience inserts us in a chain of events where the things we do and launch in our world turn back on us. In *Retrieving nature: education for a post-humanist age* (2004), Michael Bonnett explores the ethical implications of cyclic time by contrasting this time experience with

> a time so linear that in its unreturning moments objects can be at once defined and the past simply be left behind. There is a sense in which in such time we constantly escape the consequences of our living—ever focussed on 'progress' our living through linear time constantly moves us on to the next 'new' thing (...). Perhaps what is needed is that something of the sense of responsibility enforced in cyclical time, where there is no escape from the returning consequences of one's actions, to be insinuated into life in linear time such that the past may again inform the present and future—a continuity of experience being preserved. Such continuity might better reflect the character of natural space and might be characterised as 'spiral' time. (Bonnett, 2004, p. 73)

Bonnett clearly shows that responsive learning itself can accurately be conceived as a spiral process, in line with Rousseau's notion of 'natural learning': we learn from the natural consequences of our deeds in a way that connects us to our environment, past and future. In a similar vein Dieuwke Hovinga stresses 'the cyclical nature of learning about the multiform relationship between human beings and nature' (2007, p. 154; our translation).

2. From a focus on objects to a focus on interactions

Whereas a straight time line directs our attention towards an end or an object at the end of the line, a spiral movement widens our horizon in changing directions. Not the end of the line, but the line itself shows the way. We are therefore invited to shift the focus of future responsibility from objects and ends to our relations with the things in our world that determine its course. Ecological awareness should be understood as an awareness of our relations to the things in our environment that sustain our way of life, more than determined by the goals we are heading to. Thus, we may be able to keep the spiral going and bend the curve in directions which enable us to care for our habitat in the near future.

In contrast to means-end reasoning, environmental responsibility emerges from caring involvements in gardening, farming, animal care, cooking, building and nature conservation. Within these activities children are likely to experience the interactions with their natural environment in a direct, bodily and sensory way.

3. *From preventing doom to anticipating care*

In order to keep a line straight, one has to get rid of all the obstacles that get in the way. To maintain a more flexible spiral line, in contrast, one anticipates a winding circuit that is allowed to move in different directions which at present cannot be taken into account. Instead of preventing future disasters from happening, future responsibility will manifest itself in caring anticipation: caring for a nearby future that allows us to continue caring. This is precisely what Noddings implies when she states that 'The one-caring must preserve the possibility of future caring if she can' (Noddings, 1984, p. 115).

Obviously, environmental problems like climate change manifest themselves primarily in the long run of succeeding decades and ages, but environmental educators cannot keep on speculating about the range of degrees the earth's temperature will rise, the rate of ice melting and the extent to which the sea level will rise. Dwelling on alarming future scenarios like these is likely to evoke feelings of impotence and defeatism, rather than environmental care. For children and adolescents as well as for adults, it is of foremost importance to deal with the problems in a time scale in which they can be judged and dealt with. When dealing with problems of climate change, for instance, environmental educators could address their manifestations in local micro-climates—improving the quality of air, water and soil in urban environments in a way that children see, hear, smell and feel the impact on their wellness, the well-being of other people, animals, plants and landscapes.

In sum, we invite educational professionals to see child's play in nature as a point of application for appeals to caring responses. By making room for free play in natural environments, educators establish a seedbed for a lasting responsiveness to calls of natural care and future considerations. This responsiveness does not need to be utilised immediately by means of environmental lessons, but can be loosely touched upon in the formation of personal judgement and discourse competences. By understanding child's play in nature as a substratum of environmental responsibility and care, we avoid excesses of 'culpabilisation': making children feel guilty about the environmental problems that we, adults, have saddled them with. Moreover, our understanding of environmental care emerging from a playful sensitisation does not create an illusion of solubility: as if all tensions that we encounter in our relation to nature are problems that can be solved. We do, however, see child's play in nature as a precondition for environmental citizenship education, since the emerging sensitivity sustains aesthetic discernment, critical vigilance and judgement in environmental issues of public interest. By focusing on education as the primary playing and learning ground and not on every social problem that is linked to global issues of environmental concern, we counterbalance the utilisation of environmental education as a 'tool' for social change and correction of 'environmentally unsound' behaviour.

With respect to future responsibility in practical reason, we propose an Aristotelian middle way between the conservationist position, implying that every valuable thing that *can* be saved *should* be saved for posterity on the one hand, and the wishy-washy attitude of 'After us, the Deluge', on the other hand. We have to accept the vulnerability and finiteness of everything of worth—and therefore adopt an attitude of 'letting be and letting go'. At the same time, we realise well enough that we cannot let go of the few things that make our life worth living, because that would undermine the caring attachments to our life-world that constitute who we are as the 'ones caring'. Where we draw the line is inexpressible in general terms. This judgement can only be made in real-life situations in which we are involved with something particular. In these situations the *Homo ludens* attitude of active responsiveness could help us to determine where our caring sentiments spring from (see Smeyers, 2010).

Obviously, this cannot be a master plan to (dis)solve all environmental problems—many problems will remain unsolvable, some in principle, others by judgemental flaws or lack of commitment—but our suggestion of a playful responsiveness may open up an in-between space for new educational possibilities.

The ethical significance of a playful engagement with our present life-world is not at all confined to the issue of environmental responsibility. In our view, moral education in general should start from a playful desire to embrace the things that appeal to us in our life, here and now, rather than teaching self-restraint, induced by abstract moral reasoning. Such attentiveness of the educator thus builds on what the child is already affected by.

Education in nature

Having acknowledged the importance of play, it is worrying to see that the opportunities for free play in nature are decreasing in contemporary Western education. Educational research shows that children spend less time in nature (Louv, 2005). However, these studies tend to define nature rather narrowly in terms of natural reserves, while we have been focusing on nature in the broad sense. The everyday life experience of nature inevitably resides in the child's life-world. Indeed, there is a major difference between the quality of nature in the life-world of a farmer's child and the environment of a child growing up in the suburbs of Amsterdam. However, even in big cities, environmental educators have succeeded in marking out exciting footpaths in natural surroundings and creating green play areas, as well as neighbourhood farms and school gardens.

In the light of this, we think that the main educational problem is not the availability of nature to play in, but rather the opportunity to play in nature. For, obviously, the relationship between children and their life-world has been transformed into an ever more controlled and mediated relationship. Unstructured time and opportunity to play, more or less free from adult supervision, is much rarer now than it was 20 or more years ago. It is not our purpose here to give an extensive outline of the causes and roots of this loss of free time in contemporary education, but undoubtedly, the loss of free time and opportunity to play is closely related to changing priorities in contemporary education and upbringing. For instance, the growing concern of parents for their child's safety, the desire for monitoring children's development and the felt importance of efficient use of educational time have diminished these opportunities.

By way of conclusion we want to call for a revaluation of Nature Education. This dimension of environmental education should provide children with the learning environment and opportunity to play in and with nature, free from immediate educational interference, evaluation and curricular purposes. Unfortunately, the particular forms of environmental education enhancing intimate physical interaction with nature—such as Nature Education, Nature Study and Conservation Education—have been pushed onto the back burner within the framework of education for sustainable development. However, recently, we have noticed a revaluation and rise of Education in Nature. The immense popularity of Richard Louv's *Last child in the woods* (2005) testifies to a growing desire of children, parents and educators for first-hand experience in nature. So now is the time to integrate Nature Education in the school curricula, the programmes of child care institutions and leisure time arrangements. Before the hype has passed by, we have to safeguard the playful learning of future responsibility, since it is here, that children experience that the future is now.

References

Arendt, H. (1958). The crisis in education. *Partisan Review, 25*(4), 493–513.

Bell, D.R. (2004). Creating green citizens? Political liberalism and environmental education. *Journal of Philosophy of Education, 38*(1), 37–53.

Bonnett, M. (2004). *Retrieving nature: Education for a post-humanist age*. Oxford: Blackwell.

Foucault, M. (1984/1988). *The history of sexuality, Vol. 3: The care of the self*, trans. R. Hurley. New York, NY: Vintage.

Hovinga, D. (2007). *Ont-dekken en toe-dekken* [*Dis-covering and covering*]. Utrecht: University of Utrecht.

Huizinga, J. (1971). *Homo ludens. A study of the play-element in culture*. Uckfield: Beacon Press.

Hutchison, D. (1998). *Growing up green*. New York, NY: Teachers College Press.

Jonas, H. (1984). *The Imperative of responsibility. In search of an ethics for the technological age*. Chicago, IL: University of Chicago Press.

Kant, I. (1790/1987). *Critique of judgement*, trans. W.S. Pluhar. Indianapolis, IN: Hackett.

Lemaire, T. (2002). *Met open zinnen* [*With open senses*]. Amsterdam: Ambo.

Lester, S., & Maudsley, M. (2006). *Play, naturally. A review of children's natural play*. London: National Children's Bureau.

Levinson, N. (1997). Teaching in the midst of belatedness: The paradox of natality in Hannah Arendt's educational thought. *Educational Theory, 47*(4), 435–451.

Louv, R. (2005). *Last child in the woods*. Chapel Hill, NC: Algonquin Books.

Margadant-Van Arcken, M. (1990). *Groen verschiet* [*Green prospect*]. Den Haag: Sdu.

Merleau-Ponty, M. (1962). *Phenomenology of perception*. London: Routledge & Kegan Paul.

Nietzsche, F. (1883–1885/1995). *Thus spoke Zarathustra*, trans. W. Kaufman. New York, NY: Random House.

Noddings, N. (1984). *Caring*. Berkeley/Los Angeles/London: University of California Press.

Postma, D.W. (2006). *Why care for nature? In search of an ethical framework for environmental responsibility and education*. Dordrecht: Springer.

Smeyers, P. (2010). Empathy, paternalism and practical reason. Philosophy of education and the ethics of care revisited. *Journal of Philosophy of Education, 44*(1), 171–180.

Smith, P.K., & Vollstedt, R. (1985). Defining play: An empirical study of the relationship between play and various play criteria. *Child Development, 56*(4), 1042–1050.

United Nations World Commission on Environment and Development (UNWCED) (1987). *Our common future*. Oxford: Oxford University Press.

Van Gunsteren, H.R. (1992). *Eigentijds burgerschap* [*Contemporary citizenship*]. Den Haag: Sdu.

Index